TABLE OF CONTENTS

INTRODUCTION

While visiting my mother several years ago, I was surprised to see how many quilts she had completed since my last visit, as she hand pieces and hand quilts. Mom told me that she quilts just an hour or two each evening while she and Dad are watching TV.

I began to think about how I budget and spend my quilting time and how often I've thought, "I'd love to do some piecing but I just don't have time." Too often we put off sewing because we feel that we don't have enough time to make a quilt, but by working diligently in small amounts of time, after a few hours we can see great progress.

I began setting aside an hour several days a week just for piecing and was amazed at how much I could get done when quilting or sewing for just one hour a few days each week. By committing to just 60 minutes, I felt a sense of accomplishment because sitting down and sewing for one hour was fairly easy to do! My goal to sew was done and I could put everything aside and wait until I had another hour to spare.

By breaking down this book into hour-long segments, I realized that each of the quilts could easily be made in one weekend if changes to weekday routines just are not possible—hence the title.

We all have demands on our time. The only way to have more time for quilting is to find areas in your own daily routine where you can work more efficiently or delegate chores. If you're finding that you're not having enough time for quilting, think about your day as you go through it and try to determine where you can save time so you'll be able to have a bit more sewing time.

Making a quilt isn't a race. Do not feel that you have to get done exactly what the instructions indicate for one hour. You may get done more or you may get done less in your hour.

Remember to enjoy the process of piecing your quilt. Do what you can when you can and you will be pleasantly surprised at how much you can accomplish in just a weekend—one hour at a time.

Tips for Successful Quilting— One Hour at a Time

Though we'd all like to add hours to our day and days to our weekends, we cannot. We can, however, make the best use of each minute of every day.

Plan ahead! With each task during the day, think about whether you could do that task more efficiently or whether you could multitask. Any time you save during the day is time you could spend doing things you otherwise would not have time to do, like quilting!

Here are tips for using that found time to make the projects in this book:

Once you've chosen your fabrics, put them all together in a container to keep them together. Too often I've kept UFOs for so long that the fabric accidentally got returned to the stash, and when I was ready to work on the UFO, the fabric was gone!

Make a copy of the pattern (or at least make a note in which book or magazine and on what page number the pattern can be found) and keep it with your project so you don't have to waste time searching for it.

Use resealable plastic bags to store pieces that have been cut and sewn. Label the cut pieces as indicated in the directions; then label the pieces that have been sewn by the hour number so you will have everything handy and organized. Put the information (piece letter/number or hour number) on a piece of paper and slip it inside the bag so you can reuse it.

Mark off each step as you accomplish it. When you get to a stopping spot, make a note on the pattern as to what you have just completed or what will be the next step. This way, there is no wasted time trying to figure out where you left off or what you've already done.

Keep everything together! Even if you think you will be coming back to the project within a day or so, place the pattern, the unused pieces, the sections on which you have already worked, any notes, any special rulers, and anything else you may find helpful in a container that can be closed. Store the container under your sewing machine or where it can be safely left undisturbed until you are able to get back to the project.

Before you begin sewing, determine how much time you can reasonably expect to spend. Sew for that amount of time. If you continue to sew longer than you should, then you'll be rushing to get dinner on the table or laundry done and that's not fun!

To get the instructions to end at a good stopping point, some steps will take a bit more or a bit less than an hour. Do not worry that it may be taking you more or less than 60 minutes to do each step.

Remember that this is not a race! Take your time and enjoy the process of making a quilt!

Fabrics and Borders

Choosing Your Fabrics

Many of the patterns work great as stash quilts. Where one fabric has been used, maybe an ecru-on-ecru for a background, feel free to use several different ecru-on-ecru or light fabrics to make up your background. If a quilt has a dark border or dark sashing, you may use several darks if you wish. Shop your stash! You may already have the perfect fabric.

Cutting Your Fabrics

All strips and borders are cut across the width of the fabric. For example, a 2" strip should be 2" x the width of the fabric.

Do all your cutting before you start sewing. The hour-at-a-time approach assumes the pieces you need are already cut. Label and store everything (I like to use plastic zipper-type bags) so it's ready when you need it. All the cut pieces have letter designations that are referred to in the sewing instructions to make it easy to find what you need next.

Borders

Yardage is given for straight-cut borders. If you wish to miter the corners on the non-pieced borders, you will need to buy additional border fabric.

Where there are pieced borders, take all precautions to be sure your top matches the measurements given so that the pieced borders will fit properly.

Even though measurements are given for the non-pieced borders, check your own top and make sure the measurements given match the measurements of your top. If not, adjust accordingly.

For all non-pieced borders:

- Cut the strips across the width of the fabric.
- Sew the strips together end-to-end using either a straight seam or a seam at an angle.
- Measure the length of the quilt and cut two side borders to that length.
- Sew the side borders onto the quilt. Press the seam allowance toward the darker fabric or toward the non-pieced strips. Square the corners.
- Measure the width of the quilt, including the side borders, and cut the top and bottom borders to that length.
- Sew the top and bottom borders onto the quilt. Press as described above. Square the corners.

Even though you may not be ready to quilt your top, make your binding, put it into a resealable plastic bag, and label the bag with enough information that you know which binding goes with which top. Try to keep the binding with the quilt top until the top is quilted and it's time to apply the binding.

Half-Square Triangles

Begin with two squares. I like to cut my squares 1" larger than the finished size of the half-square triangle unit I'm making.

Draw a diagonal line across the lighter of the squares. With the two squares right sides together, sew a scant ¼" on both sides of the drawn line. Cut on the drawn line. Press the seam allowances toward the darker fabric. You now have two half-square triangle units.

Quarter-Square Triangles

Begin with two squares. I like to cut mine 1½" larger than the finished size of the quarter-square triangle unit I'm making. Make two half-square triangle units as described previously.

Draw a diagonal line across one of the half-square triangle units in the opposite direction of the diagonal seam line.

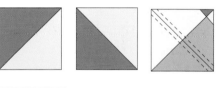

Lay the half-square triangle with the drawn line over the other half-square triangle, right sides together, carefully butting the seam allowances against each other.

Sew a scant ¼" on both sides of the drawn line. Cut along the drawn line. Press the seam allowances to one side.

Finishing

Refer to one of the many books with detailed instructions on layering, quilting, and binding quilts. Hours for finishing are not included in the project time estimates.

67½" x 88½", made by the author
Block size: 8½" finished – 9" unfinished

Judy Laquidara

FABRIC REQUIREMENTS

Ecru – ¾ yard
Gold – ¾ yard
Dark Green – 2¾ yards
Light Green – 1½ yards
Variety of Oranges, Golds, Browns, and Greens – 1½ yards total
Backing – 5¾ yards
Batting – 76" x 97"
Binding – ¾ yard

CUTTING INSTRUCTIONS

Ecru	Cut 7 – 3½" strips (A)
Variety of Oranges, Golds, and Browns	Cut a total of 7 – 3½" strips (B)
Variety of Oranges, Golds, Browns, and Greens	Cut a total of 9 – 2½" strips into 54 – 2½" x 6" rectangles (C) for pieced border #3
Gold	Cut 15 – 1½" strips (I) for Borders #2 & #4
Dark Green	Cut 5 – 5½" strips into 35 – 5½" x 5½" squares. Cut each twice on the diagonal into 4 triangles, for a total of 140 triangles (D). Cut 8 – 2½" strips (G) Cut 7 – 2" strips (H) for Border #1 Cut 9 – 3½" strips (J) for Border #5
Light Green	Cut 5 – 5½" strips into 35 – 5½" x 5½" squares. Cut each on the diagonal twice into 4 triangles, for a total of 140 triangles (E). Cut 8 – 2½" strips into 30 – 2½" x 9" sashing strips (F)
Binding	Cut 9 – 2½" strips

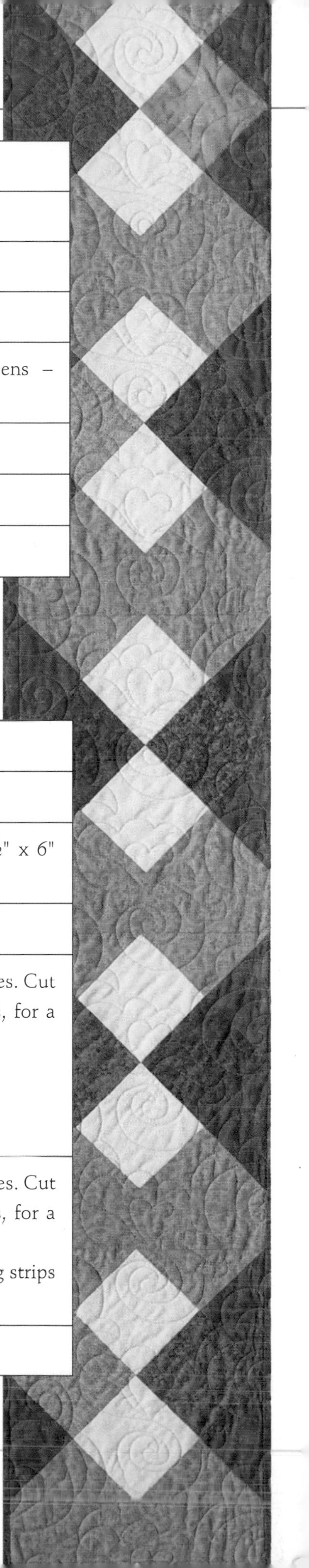

Sewing Instructions

1

Make 7 strip-sets with the 3½" ecru strips (A) and a variety of colored 3½" strips (B). Press the seam allowances toward the colored strips. Cut 70 – 3½" segments.

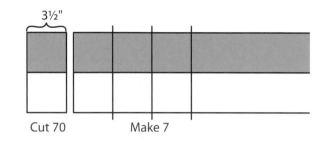

3½"

Cut 70   Make 7

Assemble 35 four-patch units as shown.

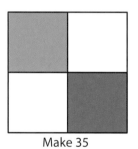

Make 35

Hour

2

Make 70 of each pieced triangle unit (140 total) with the (D) and (E) triangles.

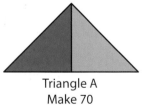

Triangle A   Triangle B
Make 70   Make 70

Sew a Triangle A to opposite sides of the four-patch units. The darker triangles should be next to the darker squares in the four-patch unit.

Hour

3

Sew a Triangle B to the remaining 2 sides of the four-patch units as shown.

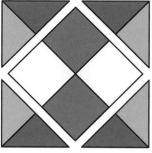

Make 35

Hour

4

Make 5 vertical rows of 7 blocks each with a 2½" x 9" light green sashing strip (F) between the blocks.

Make 5
Vertical Rows

Hour

5

Join the dark green 2½" strips (G) end-to-end and cut into 4 – 2½" x 72" sashing strips.

Join the 5 rows with the 4 dark green sashing strips. The quilt top should measure 51" x 72".

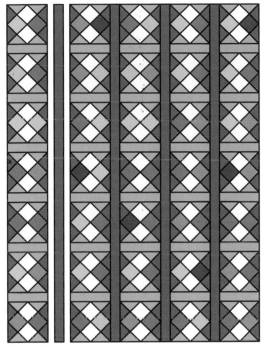

Make 2 strips of 11 – 2½" x 6" rectangles each (C) for the top and bottom borders. Cut to measure 2½" x 60" and add to the quilt. The top should measure 60" x 81".

Border #4

Join the remaining 8 – 1½" strips of gold (I) end-to-end. Cut the side borders to measure 1½" x 81" and add to the quilt. Cut the top and bottom borders to measure 1½" x 62" and add to the quilt. The top should measure 62" x 83".

Border #5:

Join the 3½" dark green strips (J) end-to-end. Cut the side borders to measure 3½" x 83" and add to the quilt. Cut the top and bottom borders to measure 3½" x 68" and add to the quilt.

Border #1

Join the 2" strips of dark green (H) end-to-end. Cut the side borders to measure 2" x 72" and add to the quilt. Cut the top and bottom borders to measure 2" x 54" and add to the quilt. The top should measure 54" x 75".

Border #2

Join 7 – 1½" strips of gold (I) end-to-end. Cut the side borders to measure 1½" x 75" and add to the quilt. Cut the top and bottom borders to measure 1½" x 56" and add to the quilt. The top should measure 56" x //".

Border #3

Make 2 strips of 14 – 2½" x 6" rectangles each (C) for the side borders. Cut to measure 2½" x 77" and add to the quilt.

BINGO WHIRL

63" x 81", made by the author
Block size: 8½" finished – 9" unfinished

WEEKEND QUILTS

12

Judy Laquidara

FABRIC REQUIREMENTS

Light Background – 2 yards
Brown – 2⅜ yards
12 fat quarters, each a different color
Backing – 5¼ yards
Batting – 71" x 89"
Binding – ¾ yard

CUTTING INSTRUCTIONS

Background	Cut 12 – 2⅝" strips. Cut 6 of these in half so that you have 12 – 2⅝" x approximately 20" strips and 6 that are the full width of the fabric (A). Cut 10 – 1½" strips into 38 – 1½" x 9" rectangles (D) Cut 5 – 1½" strips (B-1) for Border #1 Cut 6 – 2" strips (B-8) for Border #5 Cut 1 – 2½" strip into 4 – 2½" x 2½" squares (B-6). Trim the remainder of the strip down to 2" and add to the (B-8) strips.
Brown	Cut 6 – 2⅝" strips (C) Cut 1 – 1½" strip into 15 – 1½" x 1½" squares (E) Cut 1 – 5" strip into 2 – 5" x 5" squares (B-5) and 4 – 2½" x 2½" squares (B-6). Cut the remainder into 2 – 2" strips (B-7). Cut 3 – 2" strips (B-2) for Border #2 sides Cut 3 – 1½" strips (B-3) for Border #2 top and bottom Cut 7 – 1" strips (B-4) in half so that you have 14 – 1" x approximately 20" strips. Cut 6 – 2" strips (B-7) for Border #4 Cut 8 – 4" strips (B-9) for Border #6
From each fat quarter	Cut 1 – 2⅝" x 20" strip (B) Cut 1 – 4" strip. (Cut a second strip from 2 of the fat quarters so you have a total of 14 – 4" strips.)
From one fat quarter	Cut 2 – 5" x 5" squares (B-5)
Binding	Cut 9 – 2½" strips

WEEKEND QUILTS

SEWING INSTRUCTIONS

Hour 1

Make one strip-set per color (12 total) with the background (A) and fat quarter (B) 2⅝" strips. Cut 4 – 4¾" segments from each strip-set (48 total).

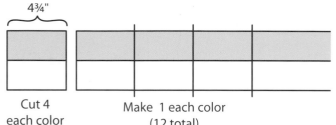

4¾"

Cut 4 each color (48 total)

Make 1 each color (12 total)

Make 6 strip-sets with full-width background fabric (A) and brown (C) 2⅝" strips. Cut 48 – 4¾" segments.

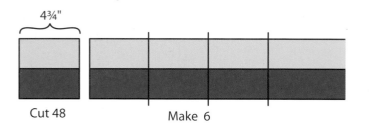

4¾"

Cut 48

Make 6

Hour 2

Make 24 blocks, each with 4 segments as shown.

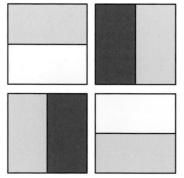

Make 24

Hour 3

Make 6 rows, joining 4 blocks together with a 1½" x 9" sashing strip (D) between the blocks, turning every other block so that the brown strips face in opposite directions, as shown. Alternate the position of the blocks on every other row.

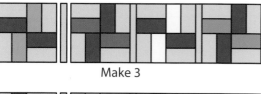

Make 3

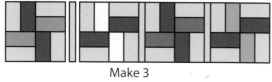

Make 3

Make 5 sashing rows, joining 4 – 1½" x 9" light background rectangles (D) and 3 – 1½" x 1½" brown squares (E).

Make 5

Hour 4

Sew the block and sashing rows together as shown. The quilt top should measure 37½" x 56½".

Border #1

Sew the 1½" strips (B-1) together end-to-end. Cut the side borders to measure 1½" x 56½" and add to the quilt.

Cut the top and bottom borders to measure 1½" x 39½" and add to the quilt. The top should measure 39½" x 58½".

Border #2

Sew the 2" strips (B-2) together end-to-end. Cut the side borders to measure 2" x 58½" and add to the quilt.

Sew the 1½" strips (B-3) together end-to-end. Cut the top and bottom borders to measure 1½" x 42½" and add to the quilt. The top should measure 42½" x 60½".

Border #3:

Make 14 strip-sets with the 1" brown and 4" fat quarter strips. Cut 102 – 2½" segments (7–8 from each strip-set).

2½"

Cut 102   Make 14

Join 30 segments side-by-side for the side borders, one starting with the brown side toward the center of the quilt and one starting with the brown side away from the center, as shown. Turn every other block in the opposite direction.

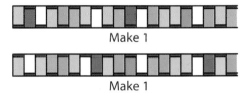

Make 1

Make 1

Join 21 segments for the top and bottom borders. Turn every other block in the opposite direction.

Make 4 half-square triangles with the brown and fat quarter 5" x 5" squares (B-5). Square-up to measure 4½" x 4½". Add the half-square triangles to both ends of the border strips.

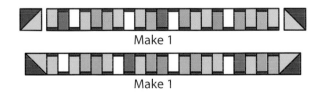

Make 1

Make 1

Hour

Sew the pieced borders to the quilt. The top should measure 50½" x 68½".

Make 8 half-square triangles with the brown and background 2½" x 2½" squares (B-6). Square-up to measure 2" x 2".

Make 8

Border #4
Sew the 2" brown strips (B-7) together end-to-end. Cut the side borders to measure 2" x 68½" and add to the quilt.

Cut the top and bottom borders to measure 2" x 50½". Add 4 brown and background half-square triangles to the top and bottom borders, positioning them as shown, and add to the quilt. The top should measure 53½" x 71½".

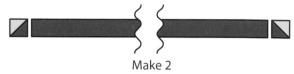

Make 2

Hour

Border #5

Sew the 2" background strips (B-8) together end-to-end. Cut the side borders to measure 2" x 71½" and add to the quilt.

Cut the top and bottom borders to measure 2" x 53½". Add the remaining 4 brown and background half-square triangles to top and bottom borders, positioning them as shown, and add to the quilt. The top should measure 56½" x 74½".

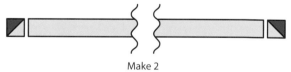

Make 2

Border #6:
Sew the 4" brown strips (B-9) together end-to-end. Cut the side borders to measure 4" x 74½" and add to the quilt.

Cut the top and bottom borders to measure 4" x 63½" and add to the quilt.

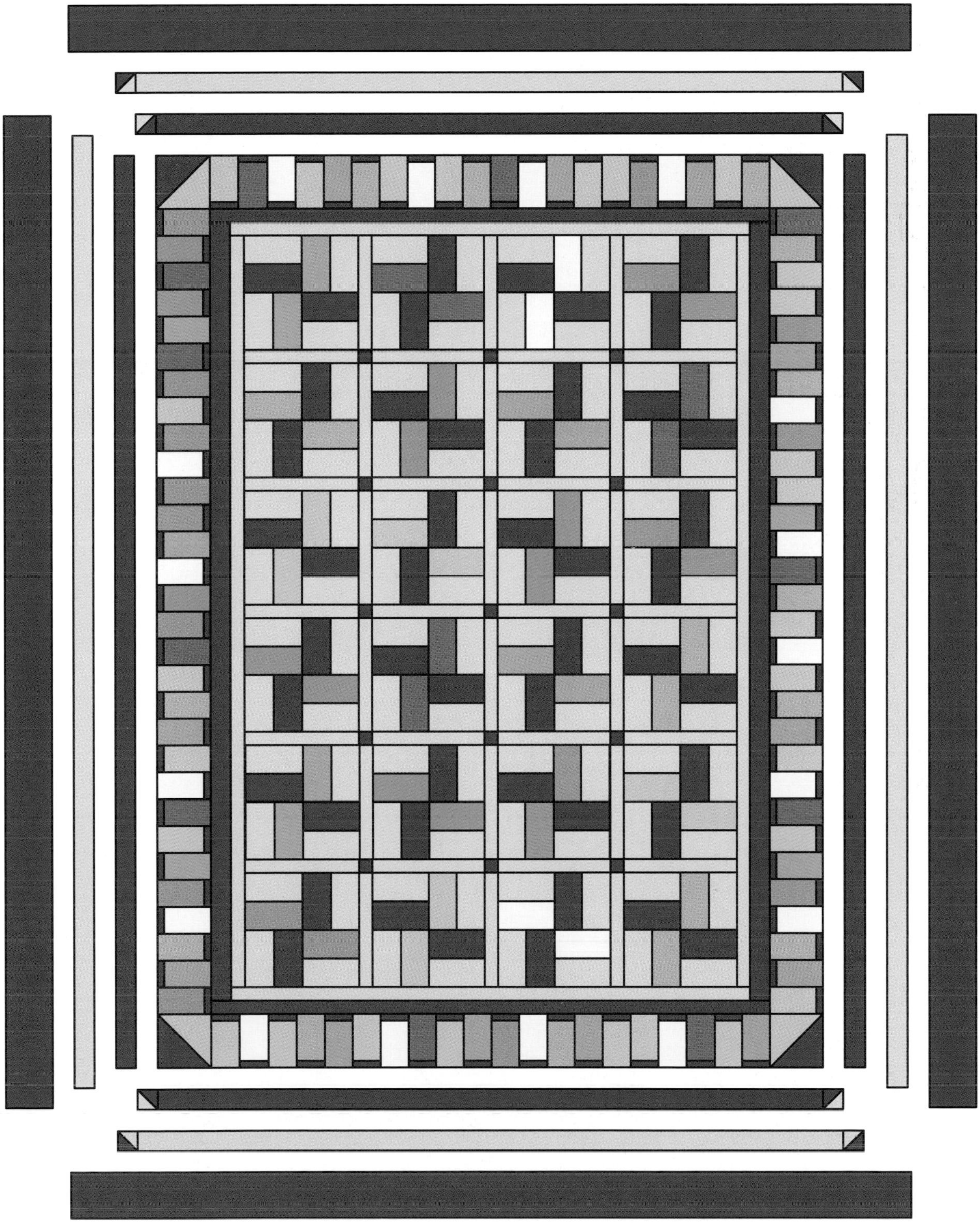

FABRIC REQUIREMENTS

Background – 2 yards
Brown – 2 yards
Light Green – 1¾ yards
Dark Green – 1¾ yards
Variety of Colored Fabric – 1⅛ yards total for the star point quarter-square triangles. You need 2 – 5½" x 5½" squares of each color so the star points in each block will match.
Backing – 7⅝ yards. Join 3 – 86" panels. The seams will go across the width of the quilt. You'll need more yardage for a directional print.
Batting – 86"x 98"
Binding – ¾ yard

CUTTING INSTRUCTIONS

Background	Cut 20 – 2½" strips (A) Cut 3 – 5½" strips into 20 – 5½" x 5½" squares (C) for the star point quarter-square triangles
Brown	Cut 20 – 2½" strips (B) Cut 3 – 4½" strips into 20 – 4½" x 4½" squares (E) Cut 2 – 2½" strips into 30 – 2½" x 2½" squares (G)
Star Points	Cut 20 pairs of 5½" x 5½" squares (D) (40 total)
Light Green	Cut 3 – 5½" strips into 20 – 5½" x 5½" squares (K) Cut 17 – 2½" strips into 49 – 2½" x 12½" sashing strips (F)
Dark Green	Cut 4 – 3½" strips (H) for Border #1 sides Cut 4 – 2½" strips (I) for Border #1 top and bottom Cut 9 – 3½" strips for the outer border (J) for Border #3
Binding	Cut 10 – 2½" strips

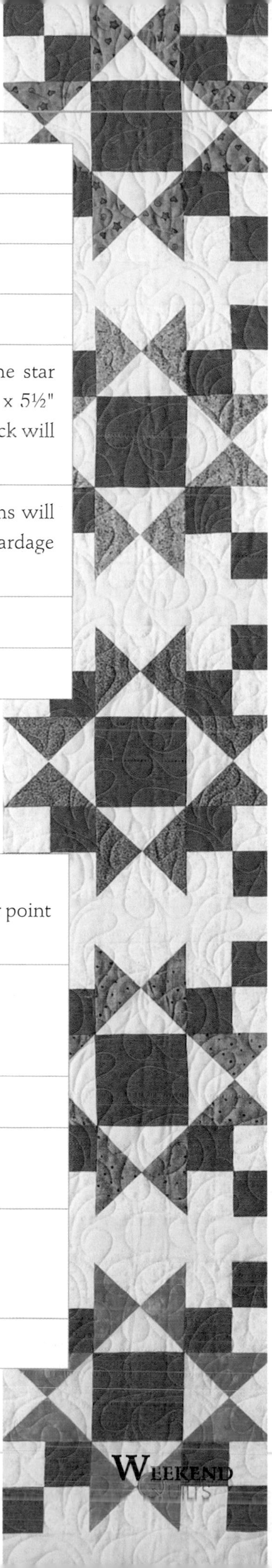

SEWING INSTRUCTIONS

Hour 1

Make 20 strip-sets with the 2½" background (A) and brown (B) strips. Press the seams toward the brown strips.

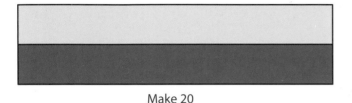

Make 20

Hour 2

Align 2 of the strip-sets right sides together with the seams abutting. Cut them into pairs of 2½" segments. Repeat, cutting a total of 154 pairs of segments.

2½"

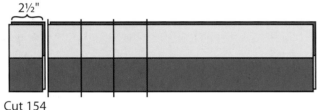

Cut 154 Pairs

Keeping the segments together as they were cut, make 154 four-patch units—80 for the blocks and 74 for Border # 2.

Make 154

Hour 3

Make 1 half-square triangle with a 5½" background (C) and star point (D) square. Make 1 half-square triangle with a light green 5½" (K) and a matching star point (D) square.

Repeat to make a total of 20 sets of 4 half-square triangles each.

Hour 4

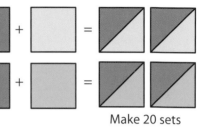

Make 20 sets

Make 4 quarter-square triangles with the half-square triangles as shown for a total of 20 sets of quarter-square triangles. Square-up to measure 4½" x 4½".

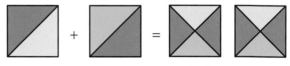

Make 20 sets

Hour 5

Make 20 blocks with the four-patch units, quarter-square triangles, and 4½" brown squares (E).

Hour 6

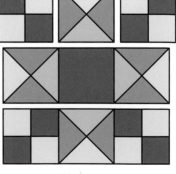

Make 20

Hour
7

Make 5 rows of 4 blocks and 5 – 2½" x 12½" sashing strips (F).

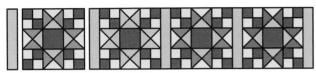

Make 5

Hour
8

Make 6 sashing rows of 4 – 2½" x 12½" sashing strips (F) and 5 – 2½" cornerstones (G).

Make 6

Sew the block and sashing rows together. The top should measure 58½" x 72½".

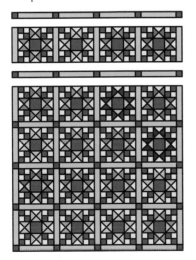

Hour
9

Border #1:

Join the 3½" strips of the dark green fabric (H) end-to-end. Cut the side borders to measure 3½" x 72½" and add to the quilt.

Join the 2½" strips of the dark green fabric (I) end-to-end. Cut the top and bottom borders to measure 2½" x 64½" and add to the quilt. The top should measure 64½" x 76½".

Hour
10

Border #2:

Join 19 four-patch units for the side borders, paying attention to the position of the dark squares. Add to the quilt.

Join 18 four-patch units for the top and bottom borders, paying attention to the position of the dark squares. Add to the quilt. The top should measure 72½" x 84½".

Make 2

Make 2

Hour
11

Border #3:

Join the 3½" strips of the dark green fabric (J) end-to-end. Cut the side borders to measure 3½" x 84½" and add to the quilt.

Cut the top and bottom borders to measure 3½" x 78½" and add to the quilt.

FABRIC REQUIREMENTS

Background – 5½ yards
Variety of 10 Colored Fabrics – ½ yard each (total 5 yards)
Backing – 5½ yards
Batting – 82" x 94"
Binding – ¾ yard

CUTTING INSTRUCTIONS

Background	Cut 2 – 3½" strips into 20 – 3½" x 3½" squares (A) Cut 30 – 1½" strips (B) Cut 5 – 2½" strips into 15 – 2½" x 11½" sashing strips (E) Cut 5 – 2½" strips (F) Cut 18 – 1½" strips for the border nine-patch units (G) Cut 3 – 2" strips (B-1) for Border #1 sides Cut 3 – 1½" strips (B-2) for Border #1 top and bottom Cut 7 – 1½" strips (B-3) for Border #3 Cut 8 – 1½" strips (B-4) for Border #5 Cut 9 – 4" strips (B-5) for Border #7

From each colored fabric	Cut 4 – 1½" strips (C) for the nine-patch units
	Cut 5 – 1½" strips into:
	    4 – 1½" x 9½" rectangles (D-1) (total 40)
	    4 – 1½" x 11½" rectangles (D-2) (total 40)
	Save the remaining strips for the pieced border nine-patch units.

Binding	Cut 9 – 2½" strips

SEWING INSTRUCTIONS

Hour 1

Make 1 strip-set per color (10 total) with 2 – 1½" colored strips (C) and a 1½" background strip (B). Cut into 16 – 1½" segments (160 total).

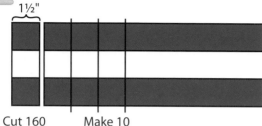

1½"

Cut 160   Make 10

Hour 2

Make 1 strip-set per color (10 total) with a 1½" colored strip (C) and 2 – 1½" background strips (B). Cut each strip-set into 8 – 1½" segments and 8 – 3½" segments.

Save the strip-set leftovers for the border nine-patch units.

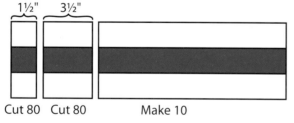

1½"   3½"

Cut 80   Cut 80   Make 10

Hour 3

Assemble 8 nine-patch units per color (80 total).

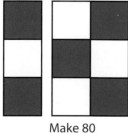

Make 80

Hour 4

Make 2 units per color (20 total) as shown with a 3½" square of background fabric (A) and forty 3½" segments from Hour #2.

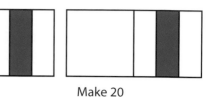

Make 20

Make 4 units per color (40 total) as shown with the nine-patch units and the remaining 3½" segments from Hour #2.

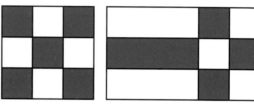

Make 40

Hour 5

Assemble 2 blocks per color with the Hour #4 units (20 total).

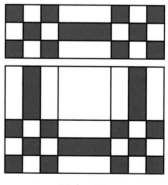

Make 20

Hour 6

Add a different color border to each block. Sew 2 – 1½" x 9½" strips (D-1) to opposite sides. Then sew 2 – 1½" x 11½" strips (D-2) to the remaining sides.

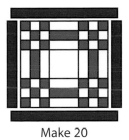

Make 20

Hour 7

Make 5 rows of 4 blocks each with 3 – 2½" x 11½" sashing strips (E) between the blocks.

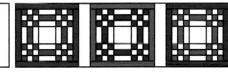

Make 5

Make 4 sashing rows by joining the 2½" strips (F) end-to-end and cutting 4 strips to measure 50½".

Join the block and sashing rows. The top should measure 50½" x 63½".

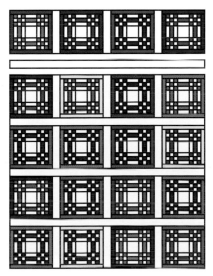

Hour 8

Make 44 nine-patch units cutting 1½" segments from the Hours #1 & #2 strip-set leftovers. Make additional strip-sets as needed with the 18 – 1½" background strips (G) and the remaining colored fabric 1½" strips (C), with background fabric in the corners.

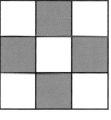

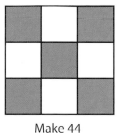

Make 44

Hour 9

With the remaining fabrics from Hour #8, make 44 nine-patch units with colored fabric in the corners.

Make 44

NOTE: The colored fabrics in the nine-patch units do not have to match. Mix them up for a scrappy look. Just be sure you have 44 with background in the corners and 44 with colored fabric in the corners.

Save your leftover 1½" colored strips for Border #2.

Border #1:

Sew the 2" background strips (B-1) together end-to-end. Cut the side borders to measure 2" x 63½" and add to the quilt.

Sew the 1½" background strips (B-2) together end-to-end. Cut the top and bottom borders to measure 1½" x 53½" and add to the quilt. The top should measure 53½" x 65½".

Border #2:

Join various lengths of the leftover 1½" strips of colored fabric end-to-end. (Cut more 1½" strips if needed.) Just whack off the lengths and don't worry about each piece being the same length. They don't need to be.

Cut the side borders to measure 1½" x 65½" and add to the quilt.

Cut the top and bottom borders to measure 1½" x 55½" and add to the quilt. The top should measure 55½" x 67½".

Make 4

Border #3:

Sew the 1½" background strips (B-3) together end-to-end. Cut the side borders to measure 1½" x 67½" and add to the quilt.

Cut the top and bottom borders to measure 1½" x 57½" and add to the quilt. The top should measure 57½" x 69½".

Border #4:

Join 23 nine-patch units, (beginning and ending with the color fabric corner units) to form the side borders and add to the quilt.

Make 2

Join 21 nine-patch units (beginning and ending with the background corner units) to form the top and bottom borders and add to the quilt. The top should measure 63½" x 75½".

Make 2

Border #5:

Sew the 1½" background strips (B-4) together end-to-end. Cut the side borders to measure 1½" x 75½" and add to the quilt.

Cut the top and bottom borders to measure 1½" x 65½" and add to the quilt. The top should measure 65½" x 77½".

Border #6:

Repeat Border #2 using the remaining colored fabrics. Cut the side borders to measure 1½" x 77½" and add to the quilt.

Cut the top and bottom borders to measure 1½" x 67½" and add to the quilt. The top should measure 67½" x 79½".

Border #7:

Sew the 4" background strips (B-5) together end-to-end. Cut the side borders to measure 4" x 79½" and add to the quilt.

Cut the top and bottom borders to measure 4" x 74½" and add to the quilt.

Think about making the binding scrappy, too!

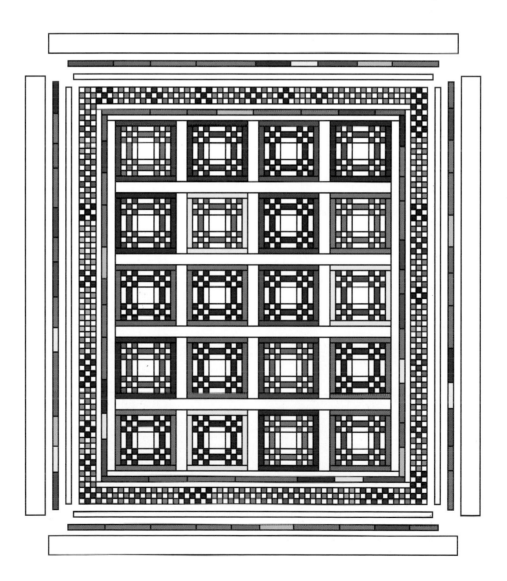

FABRIC REQUIREMENTS

Black – 5⅜ yards
Yellow – ½ yard

Colored Fabric – 14 fat quarters
    From each fat quarter, you will get 4 blocks and 5
        border blocks.

Backing – 7⅝ yards
        Join 3 – 78" panels The seams will go across the
        width of the quilt. You'll need more yardage for
        a directional print.

Batting – 86" x 106"
Binding – ¾ yard

CUTTING INSTRUCTIONS

Black	Cut 6 – 5" strips into 48 – 5" x 5" squares (A) Cut 7 – 5½" strips into 48 – 5½" x 5½" squares (B) Cut 5 – 3" strips into 60 – 3" x 3"squares (J) Cut 6 – 3½" strips into 60 – 3½" x 3½" squares (G) Cut 4 – 3½" strips (B-1) for Border #1 sides Cut 13 – 4½" strips (B-2) for Border #1 top and bottom
Yellow	Cut 4 – 3¼" strips into 48 – 3¼" x 3¼" squares (D)

From each fat quarter, cut:	8 – 2¾" x 2¾" squares (F)
	4 – 3¼" x 3¼" squares (E)
	4 – 5½" x 5½" squares (C)
	4 – 3½" x 3½" squares (H) (Cut one more from 6 of the fat
	        quarters so you have a total of 60.)
	4 – 3" x 3" squares (I). (Cut one more from 6 of the fat quarters
	        so you have a total of 60.)

Binding	Cut 10 – 2½" strips

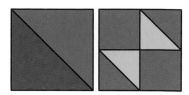

Sew a larger half-square triangle to one side of a matching four-patch unit, paying attention to the orientation of the triangles.

Fat Quarter Cutting Chart

C	C	E	I
		E	I
C	C	E	I
		E	I
F	F	F	F	E	I
F	F	F	F		I
H	H	H	H	H

SEWING INSTRUCTIONS

Hour 1

Make 96 half-square triangles with 48 black 5½" squares (B) and 48 colored 5½" squares (C). Square-up to measure 5" x 5".

Make 96

Hour 2

Make 96 half-square triangles with 48 yellow 3¼" squares (D) and 48 colored 3¼" squares (E). Square-up to measure 2¾" x 2¾".

Make 96

Hour 3

Make 48 four-patch units as shown with the smaller half-square triangles and matching colored 2¾" squares (F).

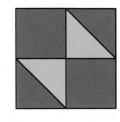

Make 48

Hour 4

Sew a 5" black square (A) to the colored side of the larger half-square triangles as shown.

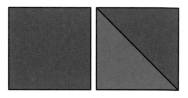

Join the two units to make the 48 blocks.

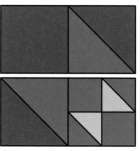

Make 48

Hour 5

Sew 8 rows of 6 blocks each as shown.

Make 8

Hour 6

Sew the rows together to complete the center of the top, alternating the orientation of every other row to make the stars. The top should measure 54½" x 72½".

Border #1:

Sew the 3½" strips (B-1) together end-to-end. Cut the side borders to measure 3½" x 72½" and add to the quilt.

Sew 4 – 4½" strips (B-2) together end-to-end. Cut the top and bottom borders to measure 4½" x 60½" and add to the quilt. The top should measure 60½" x 80½".

Hour 7

Border #2:

Make 120 half-square triangles with 60 black 3½" squares (G) and 60 colored 3½" squares (H). Trim to measure 3" x 3".

Make 120

Hour 8

Join 60 half-square triangles to matching 3" colored squares (I) as shown.

Join 60 half-square triangles to black 3" squares (J) as shown.

Join the two units to complete the 60 border blocks.

Hour 9

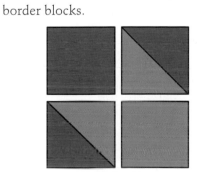

Make 60

Join 16 blocks for the side borders and add to the quilt.

Hour 10

Join 14 blocks for the top and bottom borders and add to the quilt.

The top should measure 70½" x 90½".

Border #3:

Sew the remaining 9 – 4½" strips (B 2) together end-to-end. Cut the side borders to measure 4½" x 90½" and add to the quilt.

Cut the top and bottom borders to measure 4½" x 78½" and add to the quilt.

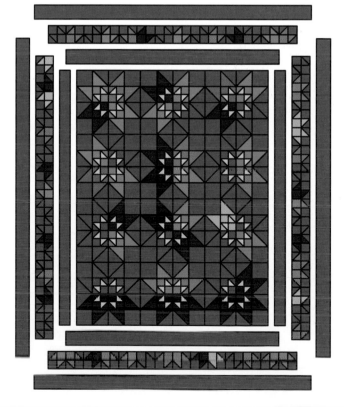

FABRIC REQUIREMENTS

Black – 3⅝ yards
White – 4¾ yards
Red – 1¾ yards
Backing – 7⅝ yards   Join 3 – 87" panels. The seams will go across the width of the quilt. You'll need more yardage for a directional print.
Batting – 87" x 105"
Binding – ¾ yard

CUTTING INSTRUCTIONS

Note: If you would prefer to use templates instead of paper piecing the blocks, do not cut pieces A, B, C, D, or E. Use the yardage to cut out the pieces using the templates (pages 37–39).

Black	Cut 10 – 6" strips into 96 – 4" x 6" rectangles (A)
	Cut 10 – 1¾" strips into 48 – 1¾" x 7½" rectangles (C)
	Cut 13 – 1½" strips (F)
	Cut 15 – 1½" strips into: 46 1½" x 5½" rectangles (I)
	                              92 – 1½" x 2½" rectangles (J)
	                              8 – 1½" x 2½" rectangles (M)
	                              8 – 1½" x 4½" rectangles (N)
	                              4 – 1½" x 1½" squares (H)

White	Cut 10 – 6" strips into 96 – 4" x 6" rectangles (B)
	Cut 10 – 1¾" strips into 48 – 1¾" x 7½" rectangles (E)
	Cut 16 – 2¼" strips (P-2) for Borders #2 & #4
	Cut 13 – 1½" strips (G)
	Cut 15 – 1½" strips into: 8 – 1½" x 4½" rectangles (O)
	                              46 – 1½" x 5½" rectangles (L)
	                              46 – 1½" x 3½" rectangles (S)
	Cut 1 – 2½" strip into 4 – 2½" x 2½" squares (K).
	Trim the remainder of this strip down to 2¼" wide and add to the strips for Borders #2 & #4 (P-2).

Red	Cut 5 – 7½" strips into 96 – 1¾" x 7½" rectangles (D) Cut 7 – 1¾" strips (P-1) for Border #1 Cut 10 – 3" red (P-3) for Border #5
Binding	Cut 10 – 2½" strips
	Make 96 copies each of the foundation paper-piecing templates Q and R (page 37).

SEWING INSTRUCTIONS

Hour 1

Lay all of the black (A) rectangles face up and cut once on the diagonal as shown. Lay all of the white (B) pieces wrong-side up and cut on the diagonal once.

Cut 96
right-side up

Cut 96
wrong-side up

Copy the foundation templates (page 37). Make 48 – 5" x 5" square units with the black (A) and white (B) triangles and the red rectangles (D).

Make 48   Make 48

Hour 2

Make 48 – 5" x 5" square units with the black triangles (A) and white rectangles (E).

Make 48 – 5" x 5" square units with the white triangles (B) and the black rectangles (C).

Make 48   Make 48

Hour 3

Make 48 pairs of units as shown.

Make 48

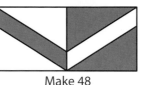

Make 48

Hour 4

Join the units to make 48 blocks as shown.

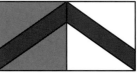

Make 48

Make 8 rows of 6 blocks each.

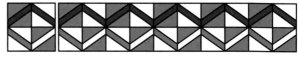

Make 8

Hour 5

Sew the rows together. The top should measure 54½" x 72½".

Border #1:
Sew the red 1¾" strips (P-1) together end-to-end. Cut the side borders to measure 1¾" x 72½" and add to the quilt.

Cut the top and bottom borders to measure 1¾" x 57" and add to the quilt. The top should measure 57" x 75".

Border #2:

Sew 7 of the white 2¼" strips (P-2) together end-to-end. Cut the side borders to measure 2¼" x 75" and add to the quilt.

Cut the top and bottom borders to measure 2¼" x 60½" and add to the quilt. The top should measure 60½" x 78½".

Border #3:

The next 7 hours are for making the 46 border blocks and adding them to the quilt.

Hour 6

Make 13 strip-sets using the black 1½" strips (F) and the white 1½" strips (G).

Cut the strip-sets into:
46 – 2½" segments
46 – 3½" segments
46 – 4½" segments.

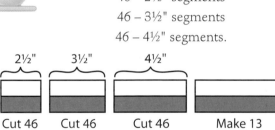

2½"	3½"	4½"	
Cut 46	Cut 46	Cut 46	Make 13

Hour 7

Add 46 – 1½" x 2½" black rectangles (J) to the side of the 2½" segments as shown. Then sew 46 – 1½" x 3½" white rectangles (L) to the black rectangle using a partial seam.

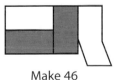

Make 46

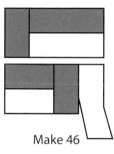

Hour 8

Continuing with the border blocks, sew 46 – 1½" x 2½" black rectangles (J) to the 3½" segments as shown.

Add to the Hour #7 units.

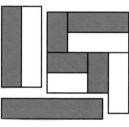

Make 46

Hour 9

Add a 4½" segment to the left side of the hour #8 units.

Add 46 – 1½" x 5½" black rectangles (I) to the bottom of the units as shown. Complete the partial seam. The border blocks should measure 5½" x 6½".

Make 46

Hour 10

For the 4 border corner blocks, make 4 units with 4 – 2½" white squares (K) and the 8 – 1½" x 2½" black rectangles (M) as shown.

Make 4

Add 1½" x 4½" black rectangles (N) to opposite sides, then add a 1½" x 4½" white rectangle (O) to one side of the units as shown.

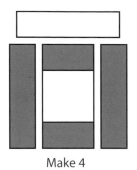

Make 4

Sew a 1½" black square (H) to one end of 4 white 1½" x 4½" rectangles (O).

Add to the right side of 2 units and to the left side of 2 units as shown to complete the corner blocks. Square-up to measure 5½" x 5½".

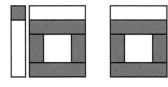

Make 2   Make 2

Hour 11

Make 2 strips of 13 border blocks each as shown and add to the sides of the quilt.

Make 2

Hour 12

Make 2 strips of 10 border blocks each. Add a corner block to each end as shown. Add to the top and bottom of the quilt. The top should measure 70½" x 88½".

Make 2

Hour 13

Border #4

Sew the remaining 9 – 2¼" white strips (P-2) together end-to-end. Cut the side borders to measure 2¼" x 88½" and add to the quilt.

Cut the top and bottom borders to measure 2¼" x 74" and add to the quilt. The top should measure 74" x 92".

Border #5

Sew the red 3" strips (P-3) together end-to-end. Cut the side borders to measure 3" x 92" and add to the quilt.

Cut the top and bottom borders to measure 3" x 79" and add to the quilt.

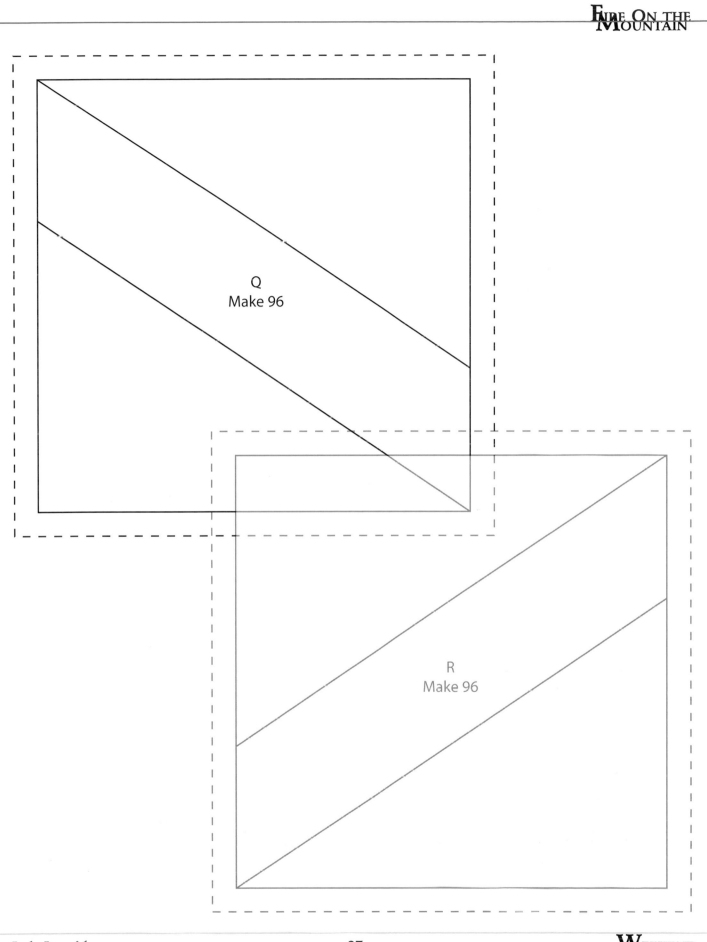

Q
Make 96

R
Make 96

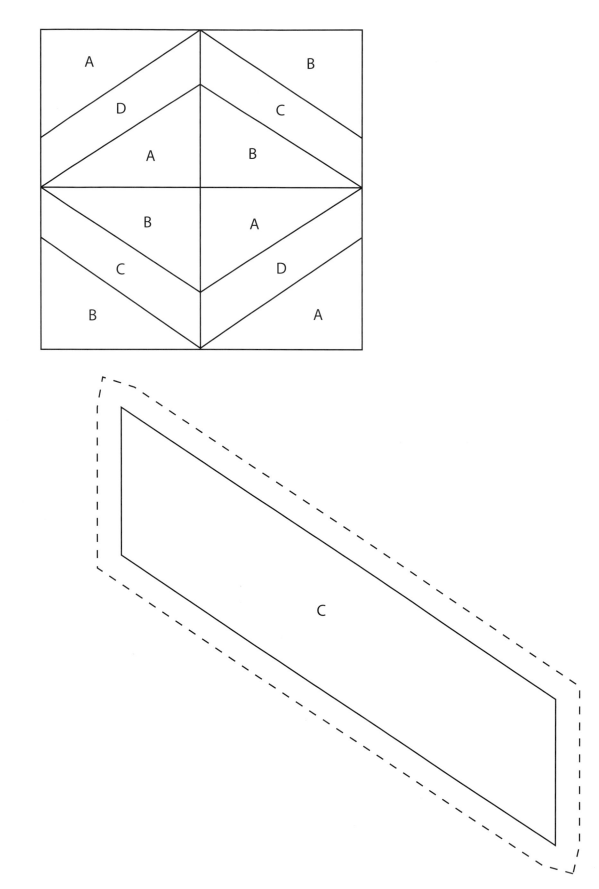

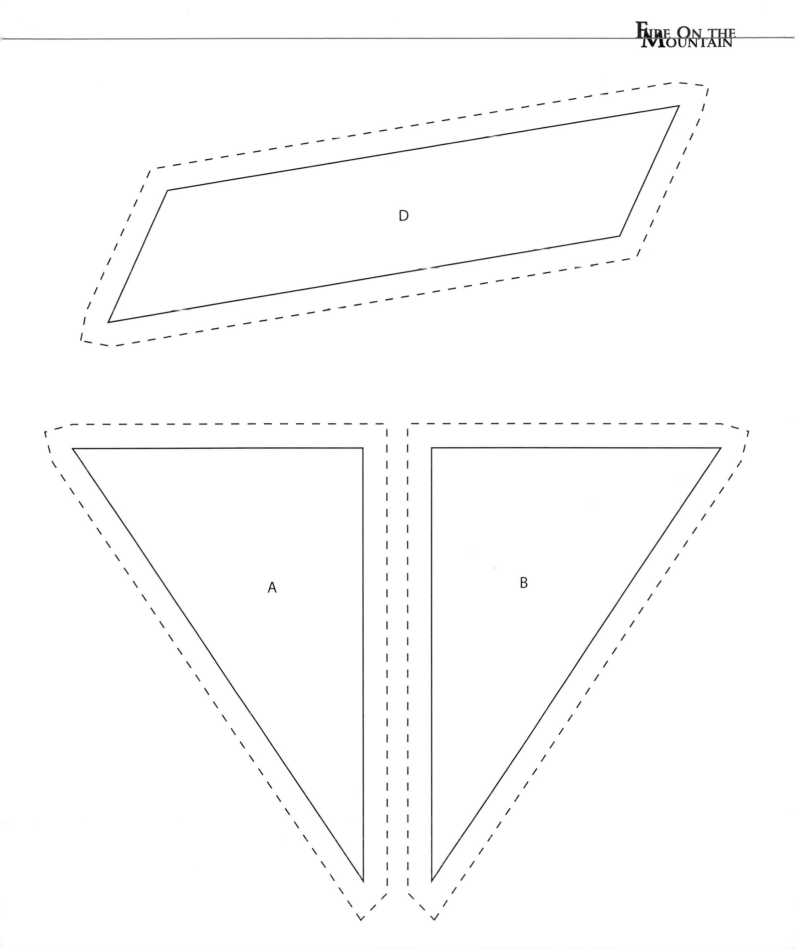

D

A

B

White – ⅞ yard	
Lavender – 3⅛ yards	
Purple – 2⅛ yards	
Scraps – 300 – 2" squares	
Backing – 5⅜ yards	
Batting – 79" x 92"	
Binding – ¾ yard	

CUTTING INSTRUCTIONS

White	Cut 4 – 3" strips into 40 – 3" x 3" squares (A) Cut 13 – 1" strips (C) Cut 1 – 2" strip into 20 – 2" x 2" squares (H)

Lavender	Cut 2 – 12" strips into:
	    31 – 2" x 12" rectangles (E)
	    18 – 2" x 2½" rectangles (F)
	    18 – 2" x 3" rectangles (G)
	Cut 6 – 3½" strips (I) for Border #1
	Cut 7 – 2½" strips. (O) for Border #3
	Cut 9 – 4½" strips (J) for Border #5

Purple	Cut 4 – 3" strips into 40 – 3" x 3" squares (B)
	Cut 13 – 2" strips (D)
	Cut 8 – 2" strips (K) for Border #4
	Cut 6 – 3" strips into:
	    14 – 3" x 12" rectangles (L)
	    4 – 3" x 8" rectangles (M)
	    4 – 3" x 5½" rectangles (N)

Various scrappy fabrics	Cut 300 – 2" x 2" squares (for the 25-patch block centers)
Binding	Cut 9 – 2½" strips

SEWING INSTRUCTIONS

Hour 1

Make 80 half-square triangles with the 40 – 3" squares of white (A) and the 40 – 3" squares of purple (B). Square-up to measure 2½" x 2½".

Make 80

Hour 2

Make 13 strip-sets with the 1" strips of white (C) and 2" strips of purple (D). Cut the strip-sets into 62 – 8" segments.

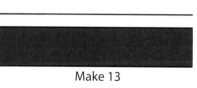

8"

Cut 62   Make 13

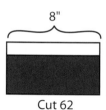

Hour 3

Add a half-square triangle from Hour #1 to each end of 38 segments from Hour #2. (You'll have 24 segments left.)

Make 38

Hour 4 & Hour 5

Make 12 block centers of 5 rows of 5 – 2" squares each.

Make 12

Hour 6

Sew the remaining 24 segments from Hour #2 to opposite sides of the 12 centers.

Add the units from Hour #3 to the top and bottom of the center sections. (You'll have 14 units left.) Press the seam allowances away from the center.

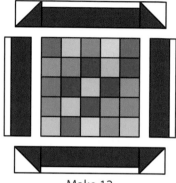

Make 12

Hour 7

Make 4 rows, each with 3 blocks, 4 – 2" x 12" rectangles (E), and a strip-set unit from Hour #3 at each end. (You'll have 6 strip-set units left.) Pay attention to the orientation of the half-square triangles in the strip-set units.

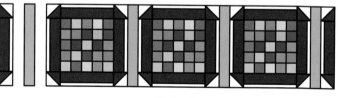

Make 4

Hour 8

Make 5 sashing rows, each with 3 – 2" x 12" sashing strips (E), 4 – 2" squares (H), and 2 – 2" x 2½" rectangles (F) at the ends.

Make 5

Make the top and bottom rows, each with 3 strip-set units from Hour #3, 4 – 2" x 2½" rectangles (F), and a half-square triangle at each end. Pay attention to the orientation of the half-square triangles. I got them backwards more than once!

Make 2

Hour 9

Sew the block and sashing rows together. The top should measure 45" x 58".

Hour 10

Border #1:

Join the 3½" lavender strips (I) end-to-end. Cut the side borders to measure 3½" x 58" and add to the quilt.

Cut the top and bottom borders to measure 3½" x 51" and add to the quilt. The top should measure 51" x 64".

Hour 11

Border #2:

Make 2 side borders, each with 4 – 3" x 12" purple rectangles (L), 5 – 2" x 3" lavender rectangles (G), and a 3" x 5½" purple rectangle (N) on each end. Add to the sides of the quilt. Press the seam allowances toward the non–pieced border.

Make the top and bottom borders, each with 3 – 3" x 12" purple rectangles (L), 4 – 2" x 3" lavender rectangles (G), and a 3" x 8" purple rectangle (M) on each end. Add to the quilt. Press seam allowances towards the non–pieced border. The top should measure 56" x 69".

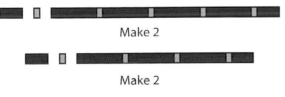

Make 2

Make 2

Hour 12

Border #3:

Join the lavender 2½" strips (O) end-to-end. Cut the side borders to measure 2½" x 69" and add to the quilt.

Cut the top and bottom borders to measure 2½" x 60" and add to the quilt. The top should measure 60" x 73".

Border #4:
Join the purple 2" strips (K) end-to-end. Cut the side borders to measure 2" x 73" and add to the quilt.

Cut the top and bottom borders to measure 2" x 63" and add to the quilt. The top should measure 63" x 76".

Hour 13

Border #5:

Join the lavender 4½" strips (J) end-to-end. Cut the side borders to measure 4½" x 76", and add to the quilt.

Cut the top and bottom borders to measure 4½" x 71" and add to the quilt.

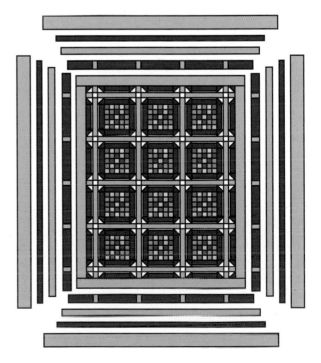

GUMDROP MOUNTAIN

71" x 89", made by the author
Block size: 10" finished – 10½" unfinished
Border block size: 3" finished – 3½" unfinished

FABRIC REQUIREMENTS

Background – 4⅞ yards
Brights – 7 fabrics ½ yard each (total 3½ yards) Seven fabrics will give you 5 blocks of each, but you may use as many different fabrics as you'd like.
Backing – 5¾ yards
Batting – 79" x 97"
Binding – ¾ yard

CUTTING INSTRUCTIONS

Background	Cut 3 – 4½" strips into 17 – 4½" x 4½" squares (A-1)
	Cut 27 – 2½" strips* into: 17 – 2½" x 6½" rectangles (D-1)
	17 – 2½" x 8½" rectangles (E-1)
	18 – 2½" x 4½" rectangles (B-2)
	18 – 2½" x 6½" rectangles (C-2)
	18 – 2½" x 8½" rectangles (F-2)
	18 – 2½" x 10½" rectangles (G-2)
*Plan your cutting carefully or you may need more 2½" strips. Optimize!	Cut 4 – 4" strips (H) for Border #1 sides
	Cut 3 – 3" strips (I) for Border #1 top and bottom
	Cut 5 – 1½" strips (K)
	Cut 8 – 1½" strips (L)
	Cut 1 – 1½" strip into: 4 – 1½" x 3½" rectangles (O)
	4 – 1½" x 2½" rectangles (Q)
	Cut 9 – 4½" strips (S) for Border #3
Brights	From each color, cut one each and that will be one set:
	You will need 17 sets of: 1 – 2½" x 4½" rectangle (B-1)
	1 – 2½" x 6½" rectangle (C-1)
	1 – 2½" x 8½" rectangle (F-1)
	1 – 2½" x 10½" rectangle (G-1)
	You will need 18 sets of: 1 – 4½" square (A-2)
	1 – 2½" x 6½" rectangle (D-2)
	1 – 2½" x 8½" rectangle (E-2)
	Cut 10 – 1½" strips (2 each of 5 different colors) (J)
	Cut 4 – 1½" strips (all different colors) (M)
	Decide which color will be your corners (I used pink).
	From that color, cut 1 – 1½" strip into: 4 – 1½" x 3½" rectangles (P)
	4 – 1½" x 4½" rectangles (R)
	4 – 1½" x 3½" rectangles (N)
Binding	Cut 10 – 2½" strips

SEWING INSTRUCTIONS

Make 17 Block A, each with the following fabrics:

Brights (use the same fabric within each block but make a variety of blocks)
1 – 2½" x 4½" rectangle (B-1)
1 – 2½" x 6½" rectangle (C-1)
1 – 2½" x 8½" rectangle (F-1)
1 – 2½" x 10½" rectangle (G-1)

Background
1 – 4½" x 4½" square (A-1)
1 – 2½" x 6½" rectangle (D-1)
1 – 2½" x 8½" rectangle (E-1)

Start by adding the B-1 rectangle to the square (A-1). Continue adding the rectangles as shown to complete the block.

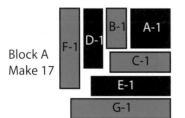

Block A
Make 17

Make 18 Block B, each with the following fabrics:

Brights
1 – 4½" x 4½" square (A-2)
1 – 2½" x 6½" rectangle (D-2)
1 – 2½" x 8½" rectangle (E-2)

Background
1 – 2½" x 4½" rectangle (B-2)
1 – 2½" x 6½" rectangle (C-2)
1 – 2½" x 8½" rectangle (F-2)
1 – 2½" x 10½" rectangle (G-2)

Use the same bright fabric within each block but make a variety of blocks.

Start by adding the B-2 rectangle to the square (A-2). Continue adding the rectangles as shown to complete the block.

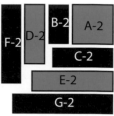

Block B
Make 18

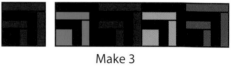

Make 4 rows, alternating 3 Block B and 2 Block A as shown.

Make 4

Make 3 rows, alternating 3 Block A and 2 Block B as shown.

Make 3

Join the rows. The top should measure 50½" x 70½".

Border #1:
Join the 4" background strips (H) end-to-end. Cut the side borders to measure 4" x 70½" and add to the quilt.

Join the 3" background strips (I) end-to-end. Cut the top and bottom borders to measure 3" x 57½" and add to the quilt. The top should measure 57½" x 75½".

Hour

Border #2:

Make 5 strip-sets, each with 2 matching 1½" bright strips (J) and a 1½" background strip (K). Press the seam allowances toward the background fabric. Cut 8–9 – 3½" segments from each strip-set (44 total).

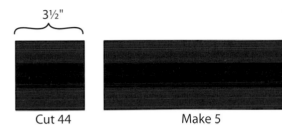

3½"

Cut 44   Make 5

Hour

Make 4 strip-sets, each with a 1½" bright strip (M) and 2 – 1½" background strips (L). Press the seam allowances toward the background fabric. Cut 10 – 3½" segments from each strip-set (40 total).

3½"

Cut 40   Make 4

For the Corner blocks, join a ½" x 3½" background rectangle (O) to a 1½" x 3½" bright rectangle (P) as shown.

Make 4

Add 1½" x 2½" background rectangles (Q) and 1½" x 4½" bright rectangles (R) as shown.

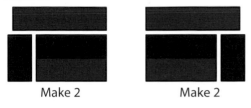

Make 2   Make 2

Add 1½" x 3½" bright rectangles (N) as shown to complete the Corner blocks.

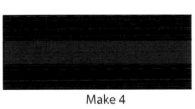

Make 2   Make 2

Hour

Make 2 side borders, alternating 13 Border Block 1 with 12 Border Block 2, as shown. Begin and end with the same color Border Block 1 as your Corner blocks. Add to the quilt.

Make 2

Make the top and bottom borders, alternating 9 Border Block 1 with 8 Border Block 2, as shown. Start and end with a different color Border Block 1 from the Corner blocks.

Add a Corner block to both ends of the top and bottom borders and add to the quilt. The top should measure 63½" x 81½".

Make 2

Border #3:

Join the 4½" strips (S) end-to-end. Cut the side borders to measure 4½" x 81½" and add to the quilt.

Cut the top and bottom borders to measure 4½" x 71½" and add to the quilt.

Just Snowballs

64" x 80", made by the author
Block size: 8" finished – 8½" unfinished
Border block sizes: 4" x 4" & 5" x 8" finished –
4½" x 4½" & 5½" x 8½" unfinished

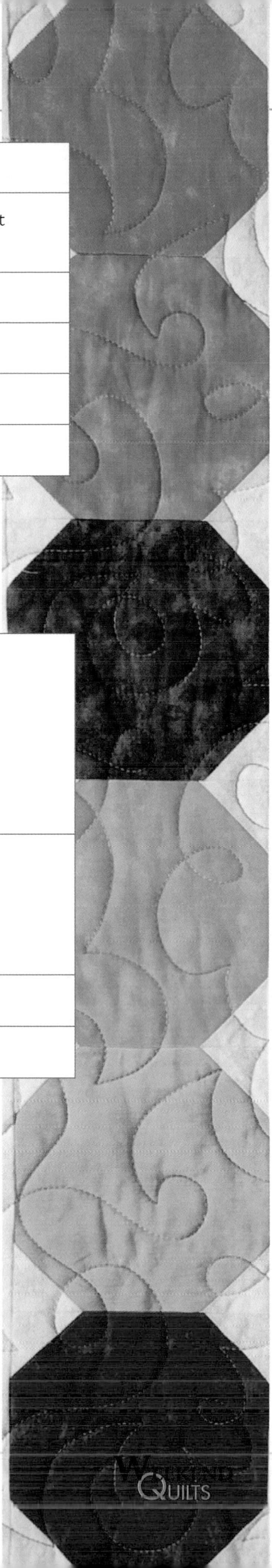

FABRIC REQUIREMENTS

Background – 2¾ yards	
Colored Fabric – ½ yard of at least 6 various bright fabrics (3 yards total)	
Outer Border – 1⅛ yards	
Backing – 5¼ yards	
Batting – 72" x 88"	
Binding – ¾ yard	

CUTTING INSTRUCTIONS

Background	Cut 5 – 3" strips into 60 – 3" squares (B) Cut 7 – 1½" strips into 160 – 1½" x 1½" squares (D) Cut 7 – 2½" strips into 112 – 2½" x 2½" squares (G) Cut 4 – 2½" strips (B-1) for Border #1 Cut 5 – 2½" strips (B-2) for Border #3 Cut 7 – 3½" strips (B-3) for Border #5
Colored Fabric	Cut 15 – 8½" x 8½" squares (A) Cut 40 – 4½" x 4½" squares (C) Cut 4 – 5½" x 5½" squares (E) Cut 24 – 5½" x 8½" rectangles (F)
Outer Border	Cut 8 – 4½" strips (B-4) for Border #6
Binding	Cut 9 – 2½" strips

SEWING INSTRUCTIONS

Hour 1

Make 15 Snowball blocks, sewing 4 – 3" background squares (B) to the corners of 15 – 8½" colored squares (A) with a diagonal seam. Trim the seam and press away from the center square.

Make 15

Hour 2

Join the blocks into 5 rows of 3 blocks each. Join the 5 rows to make the center of the top. The quilt top should measure 24½" x 40½".

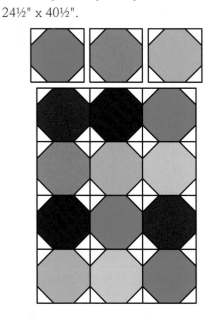

Border #1:

Join the 2½" background strips (B-1) end-to-end. Cut the side borders to measure 2½" x 40½" and add to the quilt.

Cut the top and bottom borders to measure 2½" x 28½" and add to the quilt. The top should measure 28½" x 44½".

Hour 3

Border #2

Make 40 Snowball blocks, each with a 4½" square (C) and 4 – 1½" background squares (D).

Hour 4

Make 2 strips of 11 Snowball blocks for the side borders and add to the quilt. Make 2 strips of 9 Snowball blocks for the top and bottom borders and add to the quilt. The top should measure 36½" x 52½".

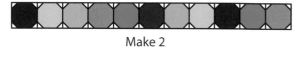

Make 2

Make 2

Border #3

Join the 2½" background strips (B-2) end-to-end. Cut the side borders to measure 2½" x 52½" and add to the quilt.

Cut the top and bottom borders to measure 2½" x 40½" and add to the quilt. The top should measure 40½" x 56½".

Hour 5

Border #4:

Make 24 "stretched" Snowball blocks, each with a 5½" x 8½" rectangle (F) and 4 –2½" background squares (G).

Make 4 corner Snowball blocks, each with a 5½" colored square (E) and 4 – 2½" background squares (G).
Make 2 strips of 7 stretched Snowball blocks and add to the sides of the quilt.

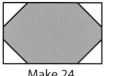

Make 24

Make 4

Make 2 strips of 5 stretched Snowball blocks with a corner block at each end. Add to the top and bottom of the quilt. The top should measure 50½" x 66½".

Make 2

Make 2

Hour

6

Border #5:

Join the 3½" background strips (B-3) end-to-end. Cut the side borders to measure 3½" x 66½" and add to the quilt.

Cut the top and bottom strips to measure 3½" x 56½" and add to the quilt. The top should measure 56½" x 72½".

Border #6:

Join the 4½" outer border strips (B-4) end-to-end. Cut the side borders to measure 4½" x 72½" and add to the quilt.

Cut the top and bottom borders to measure 4½" x 64½" and add to the quilt.

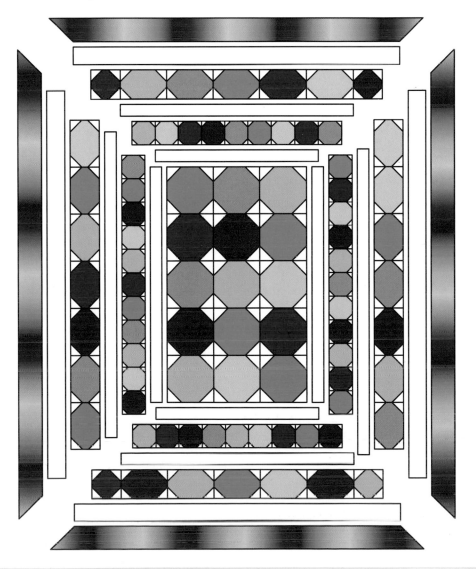

Judy Laquidara

FABRIC REQUIREMENTS

Background – 1⅝ yards	
Large variety of bright scraps – 4½–5 yards total The largest pieces needed are 4¼" x 4¼" squares for the blocks; 2" x 9½" rectangles for the sashing; and 1¼" by up to 9½" rectangles for the block borders.	
Yellow – ¼ yard	
Purple – ⅞ yard	
Backing – 5 yards	
Batting – 74" x 85"	
Binding – ¾ yard (The binding can be scrappy, too!)	

CUTTING INSTRUCTIONS

Background	Cut 4 – 4¼" strips into 30 – 4¼" x 4¼" squares. Cut the squares twice on the diagonal to create 120 triangles (A). Cut 11 – 2" strips into 120 – 2" x 3½" rectangles (B) Cut 7 – 2" strips (B-1) for Border #1
Variety of scraps	Cut 30 – 4¼" x 4¼" squares. Cut the squares twice on the diagonal to create 120 triangles (C). Cut 60 – 3⅞" x 3⅞" squares. Cut the squares once the diagonal to end up with 120 triangles (D). Cut 30 – 1¼" x 8" rectangles (E) Cut 60 – 1¼" x 8¾" rectangles (F) Cut 30 – 1¼" x 9½" rectangles (G) Cut 71 – 2" x 9½" rectangles (H) Cut 2" wide strips in a variety of lengths to make the pieced border (K). You'll need a total of 263" of border plus ½" seam allowance on each piece. These can be cut square on the ends or at an angle.
Yellow	Cut 4 – 2" strips into: 30 – 2" x 2" squares (I) 42 – 2" x 2" squares (J)
Purple	Cut 8 – 3½" strips (B-2) for Border #3
Binding	Cut 9 – 2½" strips

 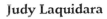

Sewing Instructions

Hour 1

Make 120 triangle units with the background triangles (A) and scrappy triangles (C).

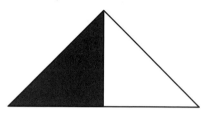

Make 120

Hour 2

Add the scrappy triangles (D) to the Hour #1 units.

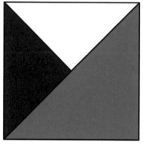

Make 120

Hour 3

Add the 2" x 3½" background rectangles (B) to one side of the Hour #2 units. Make 120.

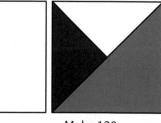

Make 120

Add a 2" yellow square (I) to 30 of the triangle units with a partial seam, as shown.

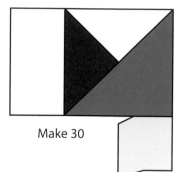

Make 30

Hour 4

Add a second, third, and fourth unit in the sequence shown, then complete the partial seam.

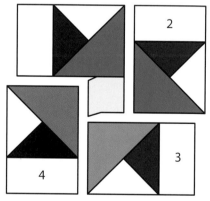

Make 30

Hour 5

Add different color strips (E, F, F, and G) around the sides of each block, Log Cabin style, as shown, maintaining the scrappy look.

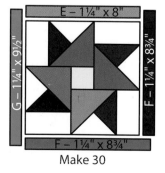

E – 1¼" x 8"

G – 1¼" x 9½"

F – 1¼" x 8¾"

F – 1¼" x 8¾"

Make 30

Hour

Make 6 rows of 5 blocks and 6 – 2" x 9½" scrappy sashing strips (H).

Make 6

Make 7 rows of 5 – 2" x 9½" scrappy sashing strips (H) and 6 – 2" yellow squares (J).

Make 7

Join the block and sashing rows. The top should measure 54½" x 65".

Hour

Border #1:
Join the 2" background border strips (B-1) end-to-end. Cut the side borders to measure 2" x 65" and add to the quilt.

Cut the top and bottom borders to measure 2" x 57½" and add to the quilt. The top should measure 57½" x 68".

Border #2:
Join the 2" colored strips of varying lengths (K) end-to-end with a diagonal seam. Cut the side borders to measure 2" x 68" and add to the quilt.

Cut the top and bottom borders to measure 2" x 60½" and add to the quilt. The top should measure 60½" x 71".

Hour

Border #3:
Join the 3½" purple strips (B2) end-to-end. Cut the side borders to measure 3½" x 71" and add to the quilt.

Cut the top and bottom borders to measure 3½" x 66½" and add to the quilt.

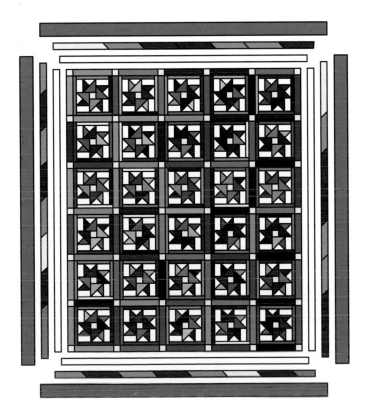

FABRIC REQUIREMENTS

4 colors for the 4 squares in the blocks – ½ yard each
Light Background – 1 yard
Dark Background – 1¾ yards
Purple – 2¼ yards
Lavender – ½ yard
Backing – 5⅜ yards
Batting – 74" x 92"
Binding – ¾ yard

CUTTING INSTRUCTIONS

Colors	Cut 4 – 3½" strips of each color into 35 – 3½" x 3½" squares (K) (140 total) 24 of each color will be used for the blocks and 11 of each color will be used in Border #3 Square #1 – Green Square #2 – Rose Square #3 – Gold Square #4 – Yellow
Light Background	Cut 1 – 7½" strip into: 24 – 1½" x 7½" rectangles (E) Cut 4 – 2" x 2" squares from the leftovers (G) Cut 1 – 2" strip into 20 – 2" x 2" squares (G, total 24) Cut 1 – 8½" strip into 24 – 1½" x 8½" rectangles (I) Cut 5 – 2½" strips (B-1) for Border #1

Dark Background	Cut 1 – 7½" strip into 24 – 1½" x 7½" rectangles (F)
	   Cut 2 – 2½" x 2½" squares from the remainder (B-11)
	Cut 1 – 8½" strip into 24 – 1½" x 8½" rectangles (J)
	Cut 4 – 2" strips into: 24 – 2" x 2" squares (II)
	                          24 – 2" x 3½" rectangles (B-3)
	Cut 6 – 3" strips (B-2) for Border #2
	Cut 8 – 2" strips (B-9) for Border #5

Purple	Cut 5 – 3½" strips into: 48 – 1½" x 3½" rectangles (A)
	                          24 – 3½" x 3½" squares (B-5)
	                          8 – 2" x 3½" rectangles (B-6)
	Trim the remainder of the remaining strip to 2½" and cut 2 – 2½" x 2½" squares (B-7).
	Cut 8 – 2" strips into: 24 – 2" x 6½" rectangles (L)
	                          60 – 2" x 2" squares (12 for half-square triangles in the blocks (C) and
	                          48 for half-square triangles in Border #3) (B-4)
	Cut 7 – 2" strips (B-8) for Border #4
	Cut 8 – 3½" strips (B-10) for Border #6

Lavender	Cut 3 – 3½" strips into: 48 – 1½" x 3½" rectangles (B) 8 – 3½" x 3½" squares (K) for Border #3 Cut 1 – 2" strip into 12 – 2" x 2" squares (D)
Binding	Cut 9 – 2½" strips

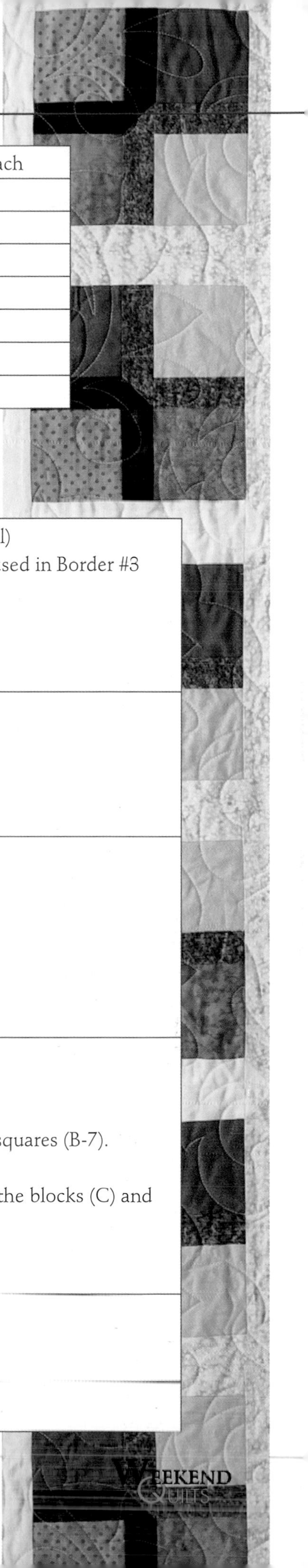

SEWING INSTRUCTIONS

Hour 1

Sew a purple 1½" x 3½" rectangle (A) between Square #1 and Square #2 (K). Make 24.

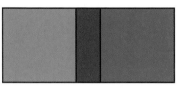

Make 24

Sew a lavender 1½" x 3½" rectangle (B) between Square #3 and Square #4 (K). Make 24.

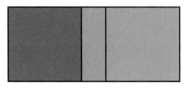

Make 24

Make 24 half-square triangles with 12 – 2" purple (C) and lavender 2" squares (D). Square-up to measure 1½" x 1½".

Make 24

Hour 2

Sew a half-square triangle between a 1½" x 3½" purple rectangle (A) and a 1½" x 3½" lavender rectangle (B). Make 24.

Join the units to make the block centers as shown. Make 24 units.

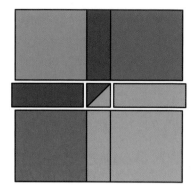

Make 24

Hour 3

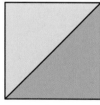

Sew a 1½" x 7½" light background rectangle (E) to the left side and a 1½" x 7½" dark background rectangle (F) to the right side of each center unit.

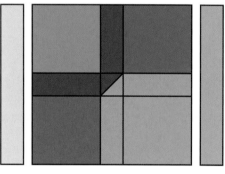

Make 24

Make 48 half-square triangles with 24 – 2" light (G) and dark background squares (H). Square-up to measure 1½" x 1½".

Make 48

Hour

4

Join a half-square triangle to light (I) and dark background (J) 1½" x 8½" rectangles as shown. Make 24 of each. Add to the top and bottom to complete the blocks as shown.

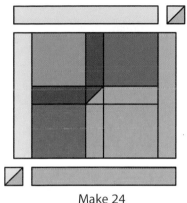

Make 24

Hour

5

Sew 4 blocks into 6 rows as shown, paying attention to the orientation of each block.

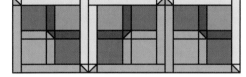

Make 6

Sew the rows together, flipping every other row. The top should measure 36½" x 54½".

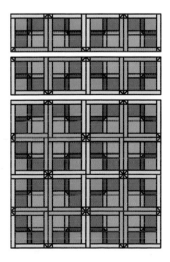

Hour

6

Border #1:
Join the 2½" light background border strips (B-1) end-to-end. Cut the side borders to measure 2½" x 54½" and add to the quilt.

Cut the top and bottom borders to measure 2½" x 40½" and add to the quilt. The top should measure 40½" x 58½".

Border #2:
Join the 3" dark background strips (B-2) end-to-end. Cut the side borders to measure 3" x 58½" and add to the quilt.

Cut the top and bottom borders to measure 3" x 45½" and add to the quilt. The top should measure 45½" x 63½".

Hour

7

Border #3:
Make 24 Flying Geese units with 48 – 2" purple squares (B-4) and 24 – 2" x 3½" dark background rectangles (B-3). Join with the 3½" purple squares (B-5) as shown.

Border Unit A
Make 24

Make 4 half-square triangles with the 2½" dark background (B-11) and purple squares (B-7). Square-up to measure 2" x 2".

Sew the half-square triangles to the ends of the purple 2" x 3½" rectangles (B-6) as shown.

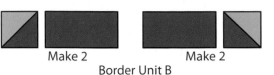

Make 2   Make 2

Border Unit B

Hour 8

Sew a 2" x 3½" purple rectangle (B-6) to one side of a 3½" square (K). Make 4, each of a different color.

Border Unit C
Make 4

Join 2 – 3½" colored squares (K) and add a purple 2" x 6½" rectangle (L) as shown. Make 24.

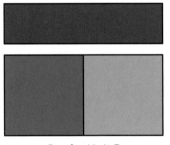

Border Unit D
Make 24

Make the side borders by alternating 7 Border Unit D with 6 Border Unit A, with 2 Border Unit B on the ends. Add to the quilt as shown.

Make 2

Hour 9

Make the top and bottom borders by alternating 6 Border Unit A with 5 Border Unit D, with 2 Border Unit C on the ends. Add to the quilt as shown. The top should measure 54½" x 72½".

Make 2

Border #4:

Join the 7 – 2" purple strips (B-8) end-to-end. Cut the side borders to measure 2" x 72½" and add to the quilt.

Cut the top and bottom borders to measure 2" x 57½" and add to the quilt. The top should measure 57½" x 75½".

Hour 10

Border #5:

Join the 8 – 2" dark background strips (B-9) end-to-end. Cut the side borders to measure 2" x 75½" and add to the quilt.

Cut the top and bottom borders to measure 2" x 60½" and add to the quilt. The top should measure 60½" x 78½".

Border #6:

Join the 8 – 3½" purple strips (B-10) end-to-end. Cut the side borders to measure 3½" x 78½" and add to the quilt.

Cut the top and bottom borders to measure 3½" x 66½" and add to the quilt.

FABRIC REQUIREMENTS

Light Background – 3⅝ yards
Dark Background – 3⅛ yards
Star Points & Pieced Border Blocks – 12 bright fat quarters
Backing – 5⅞ yards
Batting – 76" x 100"
Binding – ¾ yard

CUTTING INSTRUCTIONS

Note: If you would prefer to use templates instead of the Tri-Recs Tool, do not cut pieces D or E. Use the yardage to cut out the pieces using the templates (page 67).

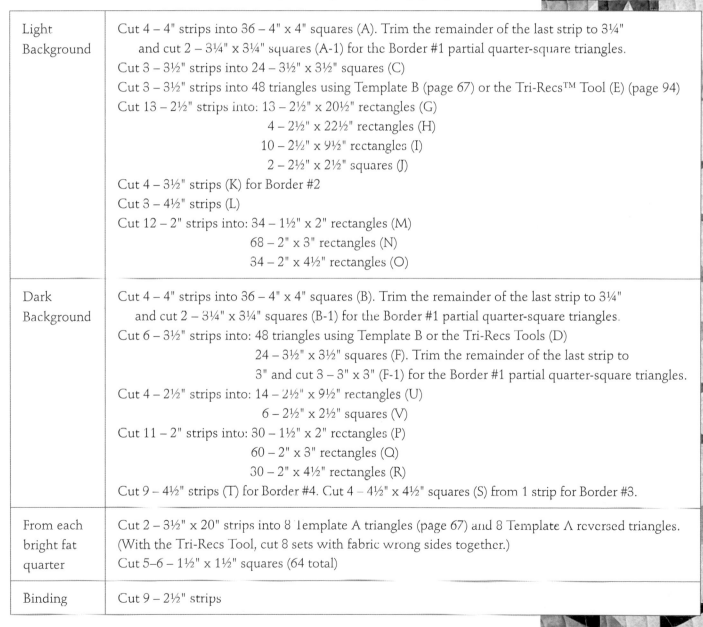

Light Background	Cut 4 – 4" strips into 36 – 4" x 4" squares (A). Trim the remainder of the last strip to 3¼" and cut 2 – 3¼" x 3¼" squares (A-1) for the Border #1 partial quarter-square triangles.
	Cut 3 – 3½" strips into 24 – 3½" x 3½" squares (C)
	Cut 3 – 3½" strips into 48 triangles using Template B (page 67) or the Tri-Recs™ Tool (E) (page 94)
	Cut 13 – 2½" strips into: 13 – 2½" x 20½" rectangles (G)
	    4 – 2½" x 22½" rectangles (H)
	    10 – 2½" x 9½" rectangles (I)
	    2 – 2½" x 2½" squares (J)
	Cut 4 – 3½" strips (K) for Border #2
	Cut 3 – 4½" strips (L)
	Cut 12 – 2" strips into: 34 – 1½" x 2" rectangles (M)
	    68 – 2" x 3" rectangles (N)
	    34 – 2" x 4½" rectangles (O)

Dark Background	Cut 4 – 4" strips into 36 – 4" x 4" squares (B). Trim the remainder of the last strip to 3¼" and cut 2 – 3¼" x 3¼" squares (B-1) for the Border #1 partial quarter-square triangles.
	Cut 6 – 3½" strips into: 48 triangles using Template B or the Tri-Recs Tools (D)
	    24 – 3½" x 3½" squares (F). Trim the remainder of the last strip to 3" and cut 3 – 3" x 3" (F-1) for the Border #1 partial quarter-square triangles.
	Cut 4 – 2½" strips into: 14 – 2½" x 9½" rectangles (U)
	    6 – 2½" x 2½" squares (V)
	Cut 11 – 2" strips into: 30 – 1½" x 2" rectangles (P)
	    60 – 2" x 3" rectangles (Q)
	    30 – 2" x 4½" rectangles (R)
	Cut 9 – 4½" strips (T) for Border #4. Cut 4 – 4½" x 4½" squares (S) from 1 strip for Border #3.

From each bright fat quarter	Cut 2 – 3½" x 20" strips into 8 Template A triangles (page 67) and 8 Template A reversed triangles. (With the Tri-Recs Tool, cut 8 sets with fabric wrong sides together.) Cut 5–6 – 1½" x 1½" squares (64 total)
Binding	Cut 9 – 2½" strips

SEWING **I**NSTRUCTIONS

Hour

Make 72 half-square triangles with 36 – 4" squares of light (A) and dark (B) background.

Make 72

Hour

Make 4 star point units of each color with the 48 Template B light background triangles (E), and 96 of the colored Template A triangles (48 total).

Make 48

Hour

Make 4 star point units of each color with the 48 Template B dark background triangles (E), and 96 of the colored Template A triangles (48 total).

Make 48

Hour

Assemble the blocks with the star points, half-square triangles, and light (C) and dark (F) 3½" squares in the corners.

Hour

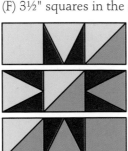

Make 24

Hour

Assemble Rows #1 and #6 as shown, alternating 4 blocks with 2 – 2½" x 9½" light background rectangles (I) and 1 – 2½" x 9½" dark background rectangle (U). Press all seam allowances toward the sashing rectangles.

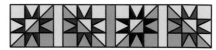

Make 2
Rows 1 & 6

Here's where we deviate a bit from what we normally do. Sew the 16 blocks for Rows #2, #3, #4, and #5 in pairs with a 2½" x 9½" dark background rectangle (U) between them, as shown.

Make 8

Hour

Make 2 sashing rows with a 2½" light background square (J) and 2 - 2½" x 9½" dark background rectangles (U) as shown.

Make 2

Join the block pairs in Rows #2 & #3 and Rows #4 & #5 with 4 – 2½" x 20½" light background rectangles (G) and the 2 sashing rows, as shown.

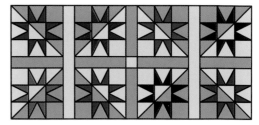

Make 2 for
Rows 2 & 3 and Rows 4 & 5

Hour

Make 3 sashing rows, each with 2 – 2½" x 9½" light background rectangles (I), 1 – 2½" x 20½" (G) light background rectangle, and 2 – 2½" dark background squares (V), as shown.

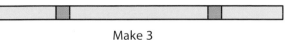

Make 3

Join the sashing rows with the block rows as shown to complete the top. Press the seam allowance towards the sashing rows. The top should measure 42½" x 64½".

Hour

Border #1:
Make 6 partial quarter-square triangles. Cut 2 light background 3¼" squares (A-1) and 2 dark 3¼" squares (B-1) twice on the diagonal to create 8 triangles. Sew 6 pairs of triangles together as shown.

Cut 3 dark background 3" squares (F-1) once on the diagonal to create 6 triangles and add to the triangle pairs to complete the partial quarter-square triangles. Square-up to measure 2½" x 2½".

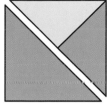

Make 6

Make 2 border strips, each with 2 partial quarter-square triangles and 3 – 2½" x 20½" light background rectangles (G) as shown. Press the seam allowances away from the partial quarter-square triangles.

Add to the sides of the quilt.

Make 2 border strips, each with 1 – 2½" partial quarter-square triangle and 2 – 2½" x 22½" light background rectangles (H), pressing as before.

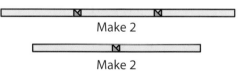

Make 2

Make 2

Add to the top and bottom of the quilt. The top should measure 46½" x 68½".

Hour

Border #2:
Join the 3½" light background strips (K) end-to-end. Cut the side borders to measure 3½" x 68½" and add to the quilt.

Join the 4½" light background strips (L) end-to-end. Cut the top and bottom borders to measure 4½" x 52½" and add to the quilt. The top should measure 52½" x 76½".

Hour

Border #3:

Make 34 light border blocks, each with a center 1½" colored square and light background pieces M, N, and O added Log Cabin-style as shown.

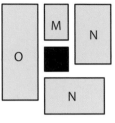

Make 34

Make 30 dark border blocks, each with a center 1½" colored square and dark background pieces P, Q, and R added Log Cabin-style as shown.

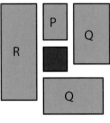

Make 30

Hour

Make 2 border strips with 10 light and 9 dark border blocks as shown. Add to the sides of the quilt.

Make 2 border strips with 7 light and 6 dark border blocks, beginning and ending with a 4½" dark background square (S) as shown. Add to the top and bottom of the quilt. The top should measure 60½" x 84½".

Make 2

Make 2

Hour

Border #4:

Join the 4½" dark background strips (T) end-to-end. Cut the side borders to measure 4½" x 84½" and add to the quilt.

Cut the top and bottom borders to measure 4½" x 68½" and add to the quilt.

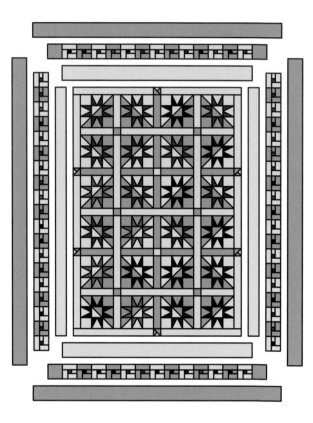

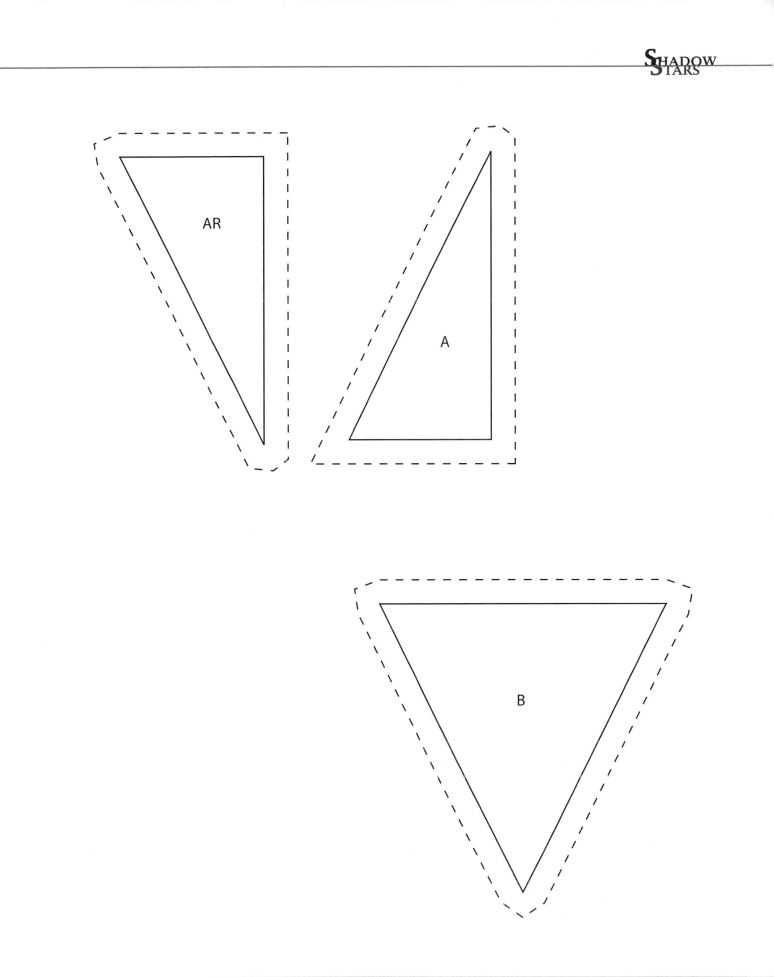

AR

A

B

Shine On Bayou Cane

FABRIC REQUIREMENTS

When choosing your fabrics, make sure that your star points fabrics (C) show up well against both your light and dark background fabrics.

Light Background – 2⅛ yards
Dark Background – 3½ yards
Variety of Scraps for the Star blocks – 2 yards total
Light Squares (A) for the Star block centers
Medium Squares (B) for triangles surrounding the center
Bright Squares (C) for the star points
Backing – 5¼ yards
Batting – 78" x 89"
Binding – ¾ yard

CUTTING INSTRUCTIONS

From Your Scraps	Cut: 2 light 3½" x 3½" squares (A) (30 total) 2 coordinating medium 4½" x 4½" squares (B) (30 total) 4 bright 4½" x 4½" squares (C) for the star points (60 total) This will give you 15 pairs of 2 identical Star blocks of each color.
Light Background	Cut 6 – 4" strips into 60 – 4" x 4" squares (D) Cut 2 – 4½" strips into 15 – 4½" x 4½" squares (F) Cut 6 – 2½" strips into 24 – 2½" x 9½" rectangles (I) for sashing Cut 1 – 3½" strip into: 4 – 3½" x 3½" squares (M) for Border #2. Cut 1 additional 2½" x 9½" rectangle for the sashing (I) from the rest of the strip. Cut 12 – 1½" strips (J) for Border #2
Dark Background	Cut 6 – 4" strips into 60 – 4" x 4" squares (E) Cut 2 – 4½" strips into 15 – 4½" x 4½" squares (G) Cut 2 – 3½" strips into 14 – 3½" x 3½" squares (H) for pieced borders Cut 7 – 2½" strips (N) for sashing Cut 7 – 2½" strips (B-1) for Border #1 Cut 6 – 1½" strips (K) for Border #2 Cut 9 – 4" strips (L) for Border #3
Binding	Cut 9 – 2½" strips

SEWING INSTRUCTIONS

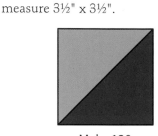

Hour 1 & Hour 2

Make 120 half-square triangles with 60 each (D) and (E) squares. Square-up to measure 3½" x 3½".

Make 120

Hour 3

Make 30 half-square triangles with 15 light background (F) and 15 bright star point (C) squares. Press the seam allowance toward the star point fabric. Square-up to measure 4" x 4". Draw a diagonal line on the backs, perpendicular to the seam.

&

Make 30 half-square triangles with 15 medium star (B) and 15 bright star point (C) squares. Press as before.

Hour 4

Layer the marked and unmarked half-square triangles, matching the center seams, making sure matching star point fabrics are opposite each other. Sew on either side of the drawn line. Cut along the drawn line to create 2 quarter-square triangles from each pair (60 total). Square-up to measure 3½" x 3½".

 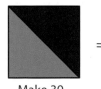

Make 30   +   Make 30   =   Make 60

Hour 5

Make 30 half-square triangles with 15 dark background (G) and 15 bright star point (C) squares. Press the seam allowance toward the star point fabric. Square-up to measure 4" x 4". Draw a diagonal line on the backs, perpendicular to the seam.

&

Make 30 half-square triangles with 15 medium star (B) and 15 bright star point (C) squares. Press as before.

Hour 6

Layer, sew, and cut as before to create 60 quarter-square triangles. Square-up to measure 3½" x 3½".

Make 30   +   Make 30   =   Make 60

Hour 7

Assemble 30 blocks (10 per hour) with the half-square triangles, quarter-square triangles, and 3½" light star center squares (A) so that you have 15 pairs of identical blocks with matching star points.

Hour 8 & Hour 9

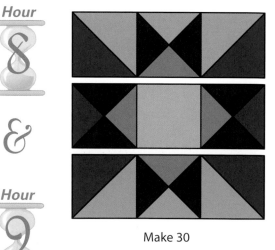

Make 30

Hour

Make 5 vertical rows of 6 blocks and 5 light background sashing strips (I) each as shown. The rows should measure 9½" x 64½".

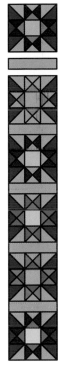

Make 5

Hour

Join the 2½" dark background strips (N) end-to-end. Cut 4 sashing strips to measure 2½" x 64½".

Join the sashing strips and vertical rows as shown. The top should measure 53½" x 64½".

Hour

Border #1:

Join the 2½" dark background strips (B-1) end-to-end. Cut the side borders to measure 2½" x 64½" and add to the quilt.

Cut the top and bottom borders to measure 2½" x 57½" and add to the quilt. The top should measure 57½" x 68½".

Hour

Border #2:

Make 6 strip-sets, each with 2 – 1½" light background strips (J) and 1 – 1½" dark background strip (K).

Cut the strip-sets into:
10 – 11¾" segments
8 – 12½" segments

11¾"   12½"

Cut 10   Cut 8   Make 6

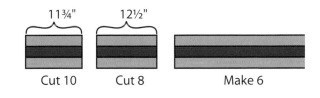

Hour

Make the side borders with 5 – 11¾" segments and 4 – 3½" dark background squares (H) as shown. Add to the quilt. The ends may need to be trimmed to achieve a perfect fit.

11¾"

Make 2

Make the top and bottom borders with 4 – 12½" segments and 3 – 3½" dark background squares (H). Add a 3½" light background square (M) to each end. Add to the quilt. The top should measure 63½" x 74½".

12½"

Make 2

Border #3:

Join the 4" dark background strips (L) end-to-end. Cut the side borders to measure 4" x 74½" and add to the quilt.

Cut the top and bottom borders to measure 4" x 70½" and add to the quilt.

FROM MY
LIME GREEN KITCHEN

Roast While You Quilt Chicken

This can be almost totally forgotten while you quilt!

4 teaspoons salt
1 teaspoon paprika
1 teaspoon onion powder
1 teaspoon dried thyme
1 teaspoon white pepper

½ teaspoon cayenne pepper
½ teaspoon black pepper
½ teaspoon garlic powder
2 onions, quartered, or 2 lemons, sliced
2 whole chickens, approx. 4 pounds each

Note: If you like this recipe, these spices can be mixed in large quantities and stored in an air-tight container for even quicker use!

Mix the first 8 ingredients. Remove any giblets, rinse the chickens, and pat them dry. Sprinkle the outside and the cavities with the spice mixture. Place either onions or lemons in the cavities and place the chickens in zipper type plastic bags. Refrigerate overnight.

Remove from the plastic bags and place the chickens in a baking dish. Preheat the oven to 250 degrees.

Bake the chickens, uncovered, for 5 hours or until the internal temperature reaches 180 degrees. Several times during baking, spoon pan drippings over chicken.

Suggestion: Roast more chickens than you will need for one meal. Leftover chicken can be pulled from the bone and used for casseroles, enchiladas, salads, or any recipe that calls for cooked chicken.

84" x 100", made by the author
Block size: 9" finished – 9½" unfinished
Border Block size: 4" finished – 4½" unfinished

74

Judy Laquidara

FABRIC REQUIREMENTS

Background– 3⅝ yards
Brown– 3¼ yards
16 assorted fat quarters (8 colors with 2 shades per color)
Backing – 8⅛ yards. Join 3 – 92" panels. The seams will go across the width of the quilt. You'll need more yardage for a directional print
Batting – 92" x 108"
Binding – ⅞ yard

CUTTING INSTRUCTIONS

Note: If you would prefer to use templates instead of paper piecing the stem, do not cut pieces E or F. Use the yardage to cut out the pieces using the templates (page 79).

Background	Cut 10 – 4" strips into: 64 – 4" x 4" squares (A) 32 – 4" x 4" squares. Cut these on the diagonal once to create 64 triangles (F). Cut 3 – 3½" strips into 32 – 3½" x 3½" squares (D) Cut 18 – 1½" strips (G) Cut 5 – 1¾" strips (B-3) for Border #2 sides Cut 4 – 1¼" strips (B-4) for Border #2 top and bottom Cut 4 – 3" strips into 40 – 3" x 3" squares (J) Cut 6 – 2⅞" strips into 80 – 2⅞" x 2⅞" squares (L) Cut 5 – 5½" strips into 31 – 5½" x 5½" squares (M) Cut 9 – 1½" strips (B-5) for Border #4
Brown	Cut 18 – 1½" strips (H) Cut 8 – 2½" strips into 124 – 2½" x 2½" squares (I) Cut 5 – 1¾" strips (B-1) for Border #1 sides Cut 4 – 1¼" strips (B-2) for Border #1 top and bottom Cut 4 – 3" strips into 40 – 3" x 3" squares (K) Cut 10 – 3½" strips (B-6) for Border #5
From each fat quarter	Cut 4 – 4" x 4" squares (B) (64 total) Cut 6 – 3½" x 3½" squares (C) (96 total) Cut 2 – 1" x 4½" rectangles (E) for the stems (32 total) Cut 2–3 – 4⅞" x 4⅞" squares (N) for Border #3 (40 total)
Binding	Cut 11 – 2½" strips

SEWING INSTRUCTIONS

You will make 32 Leaf blocks. Each Leaf block requires:

2 – 4" squares for half-square triangles made of background fabric and leaf fabric (A) and (B)

1 – 3½" x 3½" square of background fabric (D)

3 – 3½" squares of leaf fabric (C)

1 – 3½" stem square (E) and (F)

Hour 1 & 2

For the Leaf blocks, make 128 half-square triangles with 64 – 4" background squares (A) and 64 of the 4" leaf fabric squares (B). Square-up to measure 3½" x 3½".

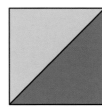

Make 64

Hour 3

Make 32 copies of the foundation template (page 78) and paper piece 32 stem units with the 4" triangles (F), and the 1" x 4½" stem rectangles (E).

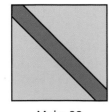

Make 32

Hour 4, 5, 6 & 7

Assemble the Leaf blocks as shown with the half-square triangles, stem units, and 3½" colored (C) and background (D) squares, mixing units with different fabrics of the same color. Make 8 Leaf blocks per hour.

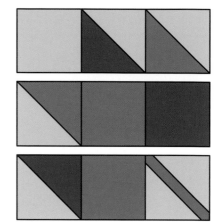

Make 32

Hour 8

For the alternate blocks, make 18 strip-sets with 18 – 1½" background strips (G) and 18 – 1½" brown strips (H). Cut into 124 – 2½" x 5½" segments.

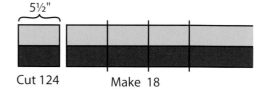

5½"

Cut 124   Make 18

Hour 9

Sew a 2½" brown square (I) to each end of 62 of the segments from Hour #8. Press the seam allowances towards the 2½" squares.

Make 62

Sew the remaining segments to opposite sides of the 5½" squares of background fabric (M). Press the seam allowances toward the center. Make 31 of these units.

Make 31

Assemble 31 alternate blocks as shown.

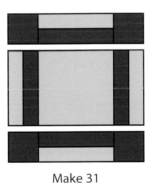

Make 31

Hour

Make 5 rows of 4 Leaf blocks and 3 alternate blocks as shown, mixing up the orientation of the Leaf blocks.

Make 4 rows of 4 alternate blocks and 3 Leaf blocks as shown, mixing up the orientation of the Leaf blocks.

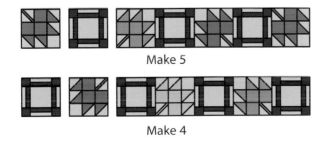

Make 5

Make 4

Hour

Sew the rows together. The quilt top should measure 63½" x 81½".

Hour

Border # 1:

Join the 1¾" brown strips (B-1) end-to-end. Cut the side borders to measure 1¾" x 81½" and add to the quilt.

Join the 1¼" brown strips (B-2) end-to-end. Cut the top and bottom borders to measure 1¼" x 66" and add to the quilt. The top should measure 66" x 83".

Border #2:

Join the 1¾" background strips (B-3) end-to-end. Cut the side borders to measure 1¾" x 83" and add to the quilt.

Join the 1¼" background strips (B-4) end-to-end. Cut the top and bottom borders to measure 1¼" x 68½" and add to the quilt. The top should measure 68½" x 84½".

Hour
14

&

Hour
15

Border #3:

Make 80 half-square triangles with 40 – 3" background squares (J) and 40 – 3" brown squares (K). Square-up to measure 2½" x 2½".

Cut the 80 – 2⅞" background squares (L) in half once on the diagonal to create 160 triangles. Attach the triangles to the leaf fabric sides of the half-square triangles as shown. Make 80 units.

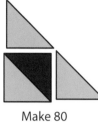

Make 80

Hour
16

Cut the 40 – 4⅞" leaf fabric squares (N) in half once on the diagonal to create 80 triangles. Sew a triangle to the 80 units from Hours #14 & #15 to complete the border blocks. Square up to measure 4½" x 4½".

Make 80

Hour
17

Make 2 strips of 21 blocks for the side borders, alternating the direction of the blocks as shown, and add to the quilt.

Make 2 strips of 19 blocks for the top and bottom borders, alternating the direction of the blocks as shown, and add to the quilt. The top should measure 76½" x 92½".

Make 2

Make 2

Hour
18

Border #4:

Join the 1½" background strips (B-5) end-to-end. Cut the side borders to measure to 1½" x 92½".

Join the 1½" background strips (B-5) end-to-end. Cut the top and bottom borders to measure 1½" x 78½" and add to the quilt. The top should measure 78½" x 94½".

Border #5:

Join the 3½" brown strips (B-6) end-to-end. Cut the side borders to measure 3½" x 94½" and add to the quilt.

Join the 3½" background strips (B-6) end-to-end. Cut the top and bottom borders to measure 3½" x 84½" and add to the quilt.

Leaf Stem Foundation Template

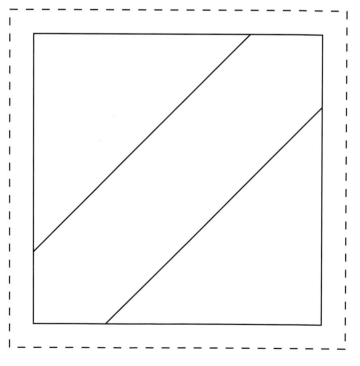

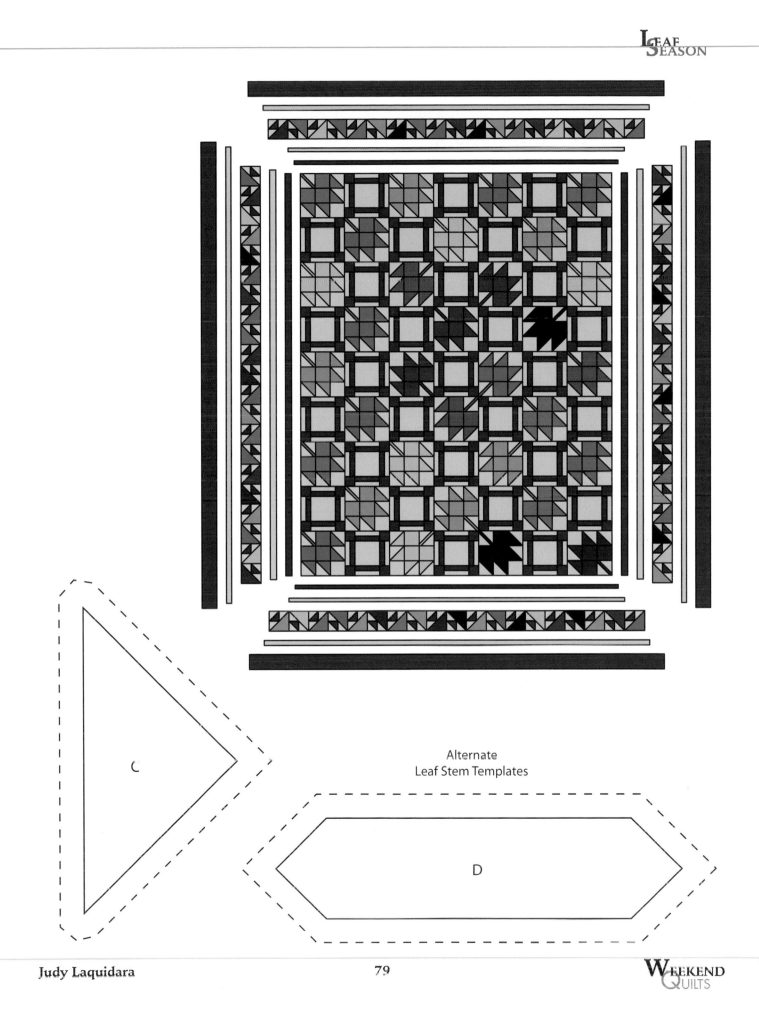

Alternate
Leaf Stem Templates

C

D

FABRIC REQUIREMENTS

Background Fabric – 5 yards	
Light Green – ½ yard	
Medium Green – 1⅛ yards	
Dark Green – 1¾ yards	
Red – 1⅛ yards	
Brown – ⅛ yard	
Backing – 7⅜ yards	
Batting – 83" x 101"	
Binding – ¾ yard	

CUTTING INSTRUCTIONS

Background	Cut 8 – 2½" strips into 62 – 2½" x 4½" rectangles (B)
	Cut 6 – 2½" strips into 62 – 2½" x 3½" rectangles (D)
	Cut 7 – 2" strips into 62 – 2" x 4" rectangles (M)
	Cut 5 – 3" strips into 62 – 3" x 3" squares (F)
	Cut 4 – 4½" strips (H)
	Cut 8 – 2½" strips (I)
	Cut 5 – 8½" strips into 110 – 1½" x 8½" rectangles (L) for sashing
	Cut 16 – 1½" strips (B-1) for Borders #1 & #3
	Cut 4 – 2" x 2" squares (B-3)
Light Green	Cut 4 – 2½" strips into 31 – 2½" x 4½" rectangles (A)
	Cut 2 – 2½" strips into 48 – 1½" x 1½" squares (K)
Medium Green	Cut 6 – 2½" strips into 31 – 2½" x 6½" rectangles (C)
	Cut 8 – 2" strips (B-2) for Border #2
	From scraps, cut 4 – 1½" x 1½" squares (B-5)
Dark Green	Cut 8 – 3" strips into 31 – 3" x 8½" rectangles (E)
	Cut 9 – 3½" strips (B-4) for Border #4
	From scraps, cut 4 – 1½" x 1½" squares (B-6)
Red	Cut 8 – 2½" strips (G)
	Cut 4 – 4½" strips (J)
Brown	Cut 2 – 1½" strips into 31 – 1½" x 2" rectangles (N)
Binding	Cut 10 – 2½" strips

SEWING INSTRUCTIONS

Make 31 tree top units, each with a 2½" x 4½" light green rectangle (A) and 2 – 2½" x 4½" background rectangles (B). Align the background pieces with the end of the green rectangle as shown. Sew on the diagonal, trim, and press. Repeat.

Make 31

In the same way, make 31 middle tree units, each with a 2½" x 6½" medium green rectangle (C) and 2 – 2½" x 3½" background rectangles (D).

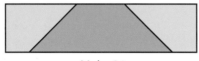

Make 31

In the same way, make 31 lower tree units, each with a 3" x 8½" dark green rectangle (E) and 2 – 3" background squares (F).

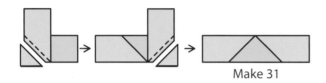

Make 31

Make 31 tree trunk units, each with a 2" x 1½" brown rectangle (N) and 2 – 2" x 4" background rectangles (M).

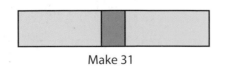

Make 31

Join all the units to complete the Tree blocks:

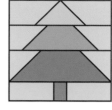

Make 31

For the alternate blocks, make 4 strip-sets, each with 2 – 2½" red strips (G) and 1 – 4½" background strip (H) as shown. Cut into 64 – 2½" segments.

2½"

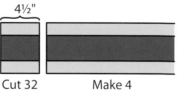

Cut 64   Make 4

Make 4 strip-sets, each with 2 – 2½" background strips (I) and 1 – 4½" red strip (J) as shown. Cut into 32 – 4½" segments.

4½"

Cut 32   Make 4

Join the strip-set segments as shown to complete the alternate blocks.

Make 32

Make 5 rows, each with 3 Tree blocks, 4 alternate blocks, and 6 – 1½" x 8½" background sashing rectangles (L) as shown.

Make 5

Hour

Make 4 rows, each with 4 Tree blocks, 3 alternate blocks, and 6 – 1½" x 8½" background sashing rectangles (L) as shown.

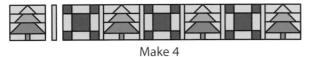

Make 4

Make 8 sashing rows, each with 7 – 1½" x 8½" background rectangles (L) and 6 – 1½" light green squares (K) as shown.

Make 8

Sew all the rows together. The top should measure 62½" x 80½".

Hour

Border #1:

Join 8 – 1½" background strips (B-1) end-to-end. Cut the side borders to measure 1½" x 80½" and add to the quilt.

Cut the top and bottom borders to measure 1½" x 62½". Add the 1½" medium green squares (B-5) to each end and add to the top. The top should measure 64½" x 82½".

Border #2:

Join the 2" medium green strips (B-2) end-to-end. Cut the side borders to measure 2" x 82½" and add to the quilt.

Cut the top and bottom borders to measure 2" x 64½". Add the 2" background squares (B-3) to each end and add to the top. The top should measure 67½" x 85½".

Hour

Border #3:

Join the 8 remaining 1½" background strips (B-1) end-to-end. Cut the side borders to measure 1½" x 85½" and add to the quilt.

Cut the top and bottom borders to measure 1½" x 67½". Add the 1½" dark green squares (B-6) to each end and add to the top. The top should measure 69½" x 87½".

Border #4:

Join the 3½" dark green strips (B-4) end-to-end. Cut the side borders to measure 3½" x 87½" and add to the top.

Cut the top and bottom borders to measure 3½" x 75½" and add to the top.

FABRIC REQUIREMENTS

White – 1⅞ yards	
Black – 4¾ yards	
Variety of colors – 9 fat quarters	
Backing – 7½ yards	
Batting – 85" x 105"	
Binding – ¾ yard	

CUTTING INSTRUCTIONS

White	Cut 5 – 5½" strips (A) Cut 3 – 3" strips (C) Cut 7 – 1½" strips (P-2) for Border #2 Cut 9 – 1½" strips (P-5) for Border #6
Black	Cut 5 – 5½" strips (B) Cut 3 – 3" strips (D) Cut 3 – 3" strips. Cut into: 36 – 3" x 3" squares (E) Cut 4 – 1¾" strips into 72 – 1¾" x 1¾" squares (F) Cut 9 – 2" strips into: 30 – 2" x 4½" rectangles (G) 38 – 2" x 4¾" rectangles (H) Cut 7 – 2½" strips (P-1) for Border #1 Cut 8 – 2½" strips (P-3) for Border #3 Cut 9 – 2" strips (P-4) for Border #5 Cut 10 – 3½" strips (P-6) for Border #7 Cut 4 – 3½" x 3½" squares (P-7) from 1 strip for Border #4

Variety of colored fabrics	From each of 9 fat quarters: Cut 8 – 1¾" x 3" rectangles (J)
	                       Cut 8 – 1¾" x 1¾" squares (K)
	                       Cut 4 – 3" x 3" squares (L)
	                       Cut 8 – 3" x 3" squares (M)
	                       Cut 3–4 – 2" x 4½" rectangles for Border #4 (N) (30 total)
	                       Cut 4–5 – 2" x 4¾" rectangles for Border #4 (O) (38 total)

Binding	Cut 10 – 2½" strips

J	J	J	J	L	L	N
						N
J	J	J	J	L	L	N
						N
K	K	K	K	M	M	N
K	K	K	K			O
				M	M	O
				M	M	O
				M	M	O
						O

Fat-Quarter Cutting Chart

SEWING INSTRUCTIONS

Hour 1

Make 5 strip-sets with the 5½" white (A) and black (B) strips. Press the seams toward the black fabric. Cut 34 – 5½" segments.

5½"

Cut 34   Make 5

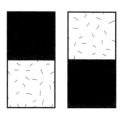

Hour 2

Make 17 Four-Patch blocks as shown. The blocks should measure 10½" x 10½".

Make 17

Hour 3

Make 3 strip-sets with the 3" white (C) and black (D) strips. Press the seams toward the black fabric. Cut 36 – 3" segments.

3"

Cut 36   Make 3

Make 36 two-patch units (4 of each color) with the 3" colored (L) and black (E) squares.

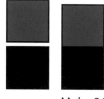

Make 36

Make 36 four-patch units with the strip-set segments and the two-patch units as shown. The units should measure 5½" x 5½".

Make 36

Hour 4

Make 72 units (8 of each color) with the 1¾" colored squares (K), the 1¾" black squares (F), and the 1¾" x 3" colored rectangles (J).

Add a 3" colored square (M) to each unit to make the two-patch units as shown.

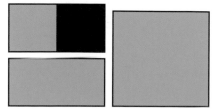

Make 72

Join into 36 four-patch units as shown, 4 of each color. The units should measure 5½" x 5½".

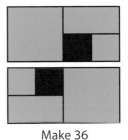

Make 36

Hour 5

Join the four-patch units from Hours #3 and #4 to make 18 color blocks as shown. Use different colored blocks but use the same colors in the center (marked A). The color blocks should measure 10½" x 10½".

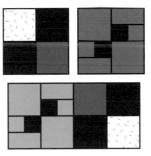

Make 18

Hour 6

Make 4 rows of 3 color blocks and 2 black-and-white blocks as shown.

Make 3 rows with 3 black-and-white blocks and 2 color blocks as shown.

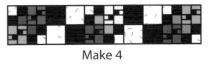

Make 4

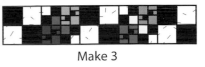

Make 3

Hour 7

Join the rows to make the center of the top. The top should measure 50½" x 70½".

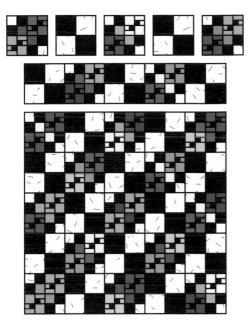

Hour 8

Border #1:

Join the black 2½" strips (P-1) end-to-end. Cut the side borders to measure 2½" x 70½" and add to the quilt.

Cut the top and bottom borders to measure 2½" x 54½" and add to the quilt. The top should measure 54½" x 74½".

Hour 9

Border #2:

Join the white 1½" strips (P-2) end-to-end. Cut the side borders to measure 1½" x 74½" and add to the quilt.

Cut the top and bottom borders to measure 1½" x 56½" and add to the quilt. The top should measure 56½" x 76½".

Border #3:

Join the black 2½" strips (P-3) end-to-end. Cut the side borders to measure 2½" x 76½" and add to the quilt.

Cut the top and bottom borders to measure 2½" x 60½" and add to the quilt. The top should measure 60½" x 80½".

Hour 10

Border #4:

Join 38 – 2" x 4¾" colored rectangles (O) to 38 – 2" x 4¾" black rectangles (H).

Join 30 – 2" x 4½" colored rectangles (N) to 30 – 2" x 4½" black rectangles (G).

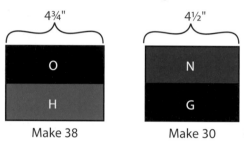

4¾"   4½"

| O | N |
| H | G |

Make 38   Make 30

Make 2 side borders by joining 19 of the 3½" x 4¾" units as shown. Trim just a little less than ½" from the 2 end blocks. This piece should measure 3½" x 80½".

4¾"

Make 2

Add the side borders to the quilt. The ends may need to be trimmed to achieve a perfect fit.

Make the top and bottom borders by joining 15 of the 3½" x 4½" units as shown .

Hour 11

Add a black 3½" square (P-7) to each end of the top and bottom borders and add to the quilt. The top should measure 66½" x 86½".

4½"

Make 2

Border #5:

Join the black 2" strips (P-4) end-to-end. Cut the side borders to measure 2" x 86½" and add to the quilt.

Cut the top and bottom borders to measure 2" x 69½" and add to the quilt. The top should measure 69½" x 89½".

Hour 12

Border #6:

Join the white 1½" strips (P-5) end-to-end. Cut the side borders to measure 1½" x 89½" and add to the quilt.

Cut the top and bottom borders to measure 1½" x 71½" and add to the quilt. The top should measure 71½" x 91½".

Border #7:

Join the black 3½" strips (P-6) end-to-end. Cut the side borders to measure 3½" x 91½" and add to the quilt.

Cut the top and bottom borders to measure 3½" x 77½" and add to the quilt.

TIMESAVING TIPS
IN THE KITCHEN

I found that I was spending the majority of my time in the kitchen, and therefore that was an area where I could save time. By organizing, planning, and cooking ahead, I've saved a tremendous amount of time and have used most of the saved time for quilting.

If you're not already working from a menu, make a menu for the entire week. Make a grocery list and go to the grocery store once! Time spent running back and forth to the grocery store is time that could be spent quilting!

In addition to using recipes that require less time in the kitchen, try making recipes that freeze well. Make extra, freeze some, and every third or fourth week, take food out of the freezer for every meal and spend minimal time in the kitchen.

Items that freeze well:
- Spaghetti Sauce with Meatballs
- Hamburger Steak with Gravy
- Sarah's Pork Roast with Gravy
- Baked Ziti
- Lasagna
- Chili
- Stuffed Green Peppers
- Sweet & Sour Meatloaf
- Taco Soup
- Twice-Baked Potatoes (Bake extra potatoes when you're serving baked potatoes and make twice-baked potatoes with the extras. They can be wrapped in foil and frozen.)

These recipes result in more quilting time. There are more at http:/www.limegreenkitchen.com.

FROM MY LIME GREEN KITCHEN

Taco Soup

2 pounds ground meat, browned and drained
16 ounces frozen corn
2 cans black beans, drained and rinsed
1 can Rotel® tomatoes
1 or 2 – 28-ounce cans crushed tomatoes
1 can chicken broth
1 cup water
1 package taco seasoning mix
1 package ranch dressing mix

Dump everything in the slow cooker and cook 8–10 hours on low. Add more water if necessary to get the desired consistency.

Serve with sour cream, grated cheddar, and corn chips.

FROM MY LIME GREEN KITCHEN

Sarah's Pork Roast
Can be cooked a day ahead!

Pork loin roast or butt
Garlic (as much as you like)
1 package Beefy Onion soup mix
2 cans beef broth
Flour or cornstarch for thickening gravy

Cut slits in the meat and insert either cloves of garlic or chopped fresh garlic.

Rub Beefy Onion soup mix over the meat. If desired, you can oil the meat a little before rubbing with the soup.

Place the meat in a baking dish and bake at 450 degrees, uncovered, for about an hour.

Remove the meat from the oven and lower the temperature to 350 degrees.

Pour two cans of beef broth over the meat. Cover with foil.

Bake for 2–3 hours.

When tender, remove the meat.

Pour the liquid into a pan. Thicken with flour or cornstarch. When the gravy reaches the desired thickness, add the meat back to the pot and simmer slowly until ready to serve. Slice and serve over mashed potatoes or rice.

FROM MY LIME GREEN KITCHEN

Crock Pot Roast Beef

1 large onion, sliced
1 beef bottom round roast (about 4 pounds)

Cover and cook on high for 5-6 hours until very tender. Remove the meat and let stand for 15 minutes before thinly slicing across grain.

Serve with either rice or as a sandwich on hard rolls.

Use the broth for gravy or for dipping.

FROM MY LIME GREEN KITCHEN

Chicken Piccata

Quick and yummy!

4 skinless and boneless chicken breasts, pounded
Salt and freshly ground black pepper
All-purpose flour
6 tablespoons unsalted butter
6 tablespoons extra virgin olive oil

2 – 14-ounce cans chicken broth
2 tablespoons capers, rinsed
⅓ cup fresh parsley, chopped
Juice of 2–3 lemons

Season the chicken with salt and pepper. Dredge in flour, shaking off the excess.

In a large skillet, melt 3 tablespoons of butter with 3 tablespoons of olive oil. When the mixture is hot, add 2 chicken breasts and brown on both sides.

Remove and set aside.

Add the remaining butter and olive oil and brown the remaining chicken breasts. Remove and set aside. They will not be done yet—only browned.

Add the lemon juice, chicken broth, and capers to the pan. Scrape the bottom to loosen the brown bits. Bring to a simmer and return the chicken breasts to the pan.

Simmer until chicken is done.

Add the parsley and serve over hot pasta.

FROM MY LIME GREEN KITCHEN

Banana Bruschetta

1 medium banana, mashed
½ cup softened cream cheese
1½ teaspoons unsweetened cocoa powder
3 medium bananas, thinly sliced
6 – ½"–¾" thick slices sweet of Hawaiian bread or any French bread

1 tablespoon butter, melted
¼ cup brown sugar
Sifted powdered sugar

Toast the bread slices and let them cool.

Combine the mashed banana, cream cheese, and cocoa powder in a medium bowl.

Spread some of the mixture over each toasted bread slice.

Place the slices on a cookie sheet.

Layer banana slices on top of the cream cheese mixture.

Brush the bananas with melted butter or margarine and sprinkle with brown sugar.

Broil the bruschetta 4"–6" from the heat for 30 to 60 seconds or until the banana slices just begin to glaze.

Sprinkle the tops with sifted powdered sugar and serve with warm maple syrup.

FROM MY LIME GREEN KITCHEN

Sweet & Sour Meatloaf

1½ pounds ground beef
1 cup dry bread crumbs
1 teaspoon salt
¼ teaspoon ground black pepper
2 eggs
½ onion, chopped

1 (15 ounce) can tomato sauce
2 tablespoons brown sugar
2 teaspoons prepared mustard
½ cup white sugar
2 tablespoons cider vinegar

Preheat the oven to 350 degrees.

In a large bowl, combine the ground beef, bread crumbs, salt, ground black pepper, eggs, onion, and ½ can of the tomato sauce. Mix together well and place into a 5" x 9" loaf pan.

Push the meatloaf down into the pan forming a well for the sauce around all the edges. Bake at 350 degrees for 40 minutes.

While the meat loaf is cooking, combine the remaining tomato sauce, brown sugar, vinegar, white sugar, and mustard in a small saucepan. Bring to a boil over medium heat, then remove from the heat.

After 40 minutes, remove the meatloaf from the oven and pour the sauce over the top.

Return to the oven and bake at 350 degrees for 20 minutes more. Let sit 5 minutes before removing from the pan.

FROM MY LIME GREEN KITCHEN

Overnight Peach French Toast

1 cup packed brown sugar
1 stick butter
2 tablespoons water
1 29-ounce can sliced peaches, drained
12 slices day-old French bread, sliced ¾" thick

5 eggs
1½ cups milk
1 teaspoon vanilla
ground cinnamon

Bring the water, brown sugar, and butter to a boil. Remove from heat and pour into a 9" x 13" greased baking dish. After the brown sugar/butter mixture has cooled a bit, add the sliced peaches. Place the bread slices on top.

Mix the eggs, milk, and vanilla. Pour over the bread. Cover and place in the fridge overnight.

Remove from the fridge and leave sitting on the counter for 30 minutes.

Preheat the oven to 350 degrees.

Sprinkle the top with ground cinnamon.

Cover and bake for 20 minutes.

Remove the cover and bake for an additional 30–35 minutes.

Serve with whipped cream and/or maple syrup.

RESOURCES

Baptist Fan Template from Circle Lord
http://www.loriclesquilting.com

Dawn Ramirez
Pajama Quilter
http://www.pajamaquilter.com

The Electric Quilt Company
419 Gould Street, Suite 2
Bowling Green, OH 43402 –3047
http://www.electricquilt.com

Meredith England
http://www.goldenthreads.com

Moda Fabrics
www.unitednotions.com

Tri-Recs™ Tools
http://www.ezquilt.com

Willow Leaf Studio
http://www.willowleafstudio.com

Judy Laquidara has been quilting since the early 1980s. Though she started out as a hand piecer and hand quilter, all of Judy's quilts are now machine pieced and machine quilted. Judy says there are too many ideas bouncing around in her head and by doing everything on the machine, she is able to get more quilts made.

Judy enjoys traveling and teaching but also loves working alone in her basement studio. In addition to quilting, Judy loves to cook and garden.

Currently, Judy lives in Nevada, Missouri, with her husband, son, mini-dachshund, a flock of assorted chickens, and the occasional deer. Learn more about Judy by visiting her blog at http://www.patchworktimes.com.

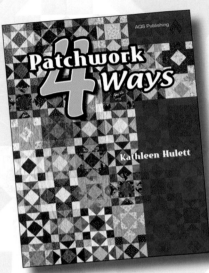

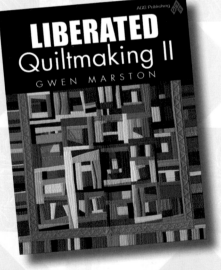